Blueprints of Success

A Reset for My Construction Business Journey

Timothy L. Wingate Jr., EA

CONTENTS

DEDICATION

To my mother, Marian Wingate, who lost her battle with scleroderma at the age of 57 and went home to be with the Lord on October 12, 2023.

To my wife, Erice, and my three boys—Timothy III, Isaiah, and David—your love and support keep me grounded.

And to my sounding board: my father, TL Wingate Sr., John Kelley, and Malcolm Haile Jr.—thank you for your wisdom, encouragement, and belief in me.

FOREWORD

From the very beginning, Timothy was special. He was a beautiful child who grew into a confident, handsome young man, now blessed with a beautiful family of his own. But beyond appearances, Timothy is a man of deep conviction, unwavering integrity, and exceptional character. He is, above all, a man of God.

A proud graduate of the University of South Florida with a Bachelor of Science in Finance, Timothy has gone on to become an Enrolled Agent with the IRS, a member of the Intuit Tax Council, and a powerful motivational speaker. He is a product of love—raised by parents who poured into him with intention, faith, and discipline. And yes, I have the honor of calling him my son.

As for me, I am a Florida State Certified General Contractor, deeply rooted in all phases of construction. More importantly, I am a man of faith who believes in Jesus Christ, the Son of the true and living God. With over 40 years of experience in the construction industry, I can confidently say: this book is a game-changer.

What Timothy has compiled here is a treasure trove of insight, guidance, and practical wisdom. It's not only a blueprint for launching a successful construction business but also a universal guide to building and sustaining any business the right way—from the ground up. If I had access to this kind of knowledge when I started out decades ago, the trajectory of my business would have been very different. I might very well be a billionaire today.

Reading this book, I was reminded of all the times Timothy accompanied me on job sites, quietly observing, absorbing, and learning. I didn't realize then just how much he was taking in. He was a sponge, soaking up the lessons of the field—and now, he's pouring them back out for the benefit of others. What he has created here is powerful, practical, and packed with tools every contractor or aspiring entrepreneur needs.

This book will walk you through the construction business from beginning to end, whether you're brand new to the industry or already a seasoned professional. It offers more than just theory—it gives you systems, tools, and actionable strategies. It teaches you how to manage people, run payroll, utilize digital tools like BuilderTrend, Gusto, and Dext—and most importantly, how to build a business that's not just profitable, but sustainable.

As a father, I'm proud. As a contractor, I'm inspired. Today, the teacher has become the student. I'm now learning from Timothy—how to operate more efficiently, how to install systems instead of relying on events, and how to equip employees with tools and resources that lead to long-term success.

You're about to be enlightened. You're about to gain access to the mind of a financial expert, a construction accountant, an IRS Enrolled Agent, and a true visionary in the industry.

Read this book with intention. Learn from it. Apply it. You won't regret it.

—Timothy L. Wingate Sr., Florida State Certified General Contractor, Master Builder & Construction Industry Veteran, Founder, Wingate Corporation LLC, Father of the Author

INTRODUCTION

This isn't your typical business book.

You won't find rigid frameworks or abstract theories that sound impressive but fall apart the moment they meet real-world challenges. Instead, these pages hold something far more valuable: hard-won wisdom from both sides of the construction industry—as the son of a general contractor and as a financial advisor who has guided countless construction businesses through their toughest moments.

My father started building his construction business in 1984, and I grew up watching it take shape. I've witnessed the exhilaration when projects finished on time and clients were delighted. I've also seen his desk covered with invoices late at night, the tension in his shoulders as he calculated whether he could make payroll, and the endless phone calls that interrupted our family vacations. Even when we were supposedly "getting away," my father was never truly present—his mind was back on the job sites, worrying about what might be going wrong in his absence.

That's not the life I want for you or your family.

Over my 15 years serving as both CFO and President across various companies, I've developed a unique perspective that few accountants can offer. I haven't just studied construction businesses—I've lived through their cycles of feast and famine. I understand that behind every spreadsheet and project timeline is a family hoping for security and a future worth building.

Since COVID, we've all gained a deeper appreciation for just how essential the construction industry is to our nation and world. Yet many of the hardest-working contractors—the ones building our communities—struggle to enjoy the fruits of their labor. They pour everything into their businesses but often have little to show for it beyond chronic stress and uncertainty.

The reason isn't a lack of skill or dedication. The problem is a lack of good data and systems that can transform raw effort into sustainable success.

Small construction companies deserve better. The founders who wake up before dawn, who carry the weight of employee livelihoods on their shoulders, who miss their children's baseball games to finish a project on time—they deserve to build something that serves their lives, not consumes them.

This book represents my commitment to modernizing the construction industry, particularly for small businesses that form the backbone of our communities. Through stories, practical guidance, and honest reflection, I'll show you how to create a construction business that doesn't require your constant presence to thrive—one that generates wealth for your family while allowing you the freedom to actually *enjoy it*.

I wrote this with a special audience in mind: not just construction business owners, but their sons, daughters, and spouses. Because I know what it's like to be the child whose parent is physically present but mentally still at work. I know what it's like to see someone you love pour everything into building something for others while neglecting to build a life for themselves.

That's why I encourage you to make this book mandatory reading for your entire construction team and new hires. When everyone understands how their role contributes to a well-organized, systematized operation, the benefits extend beyond the bottom line to touch every aspect of your life and the lives of those you care about.

The pages that follow contain the blueprint for a different kind of construction business—one that works *for* you instead of demanding everything *from* you. It's time to build something that stands even when you step away to enjoy the life you've worked so hard to create.

Let's get started.

Timothy L. Wingate Jr., EA

CHAPTER 1

MEMORIES OF THE FIRST BUILD

Looking back, I see how all these issues were interconnected. The chaos in the back office spilled over into the field, creating a ripple effect that touched every part of the business. Poor financial management led to cash flow problems, which made it harder to pay vendors and meet deadlines. Missed deadlines eroded trust with clients, which made it harder to win new jobs. It was a vicious cycle, and I was too inexperienced to break it.

The final blow came when I couldn't make payroll. I had always promised myself I'd take care of my team, but that week, I couldn't deliver. Watching them walk away, knowing I had let them down, was one of the hardest moments of my life.

That was the day I knew the business needed a complete overhaul. But it was also the day I realized something had to change—starting with me.

When I think back on that remodel job, I can still feel the sting of failure. What started as a simple kitchen renovation spiraled into a mess of delays and extra costs. The client had asked for a few changes—moving the sink to a different wall, adding recessed lighting in the living room—and I naively said, "Sure, no problem." I didn't charge for the changes up front because, honestly, I didn't know how. I was afraid they'd think I was nickel-and-diming them, so I told myself I'd "figure it out later."

Later never came. Instead, my crew was left scrambling to implement last-minute changes without a clear plan, while I was busy trying to juggle materials we didn't budget for and subcontractors who were annoyed about the shifting schedule. The homeowner, understandably, grew frustrated. By the time the project wrapped up, they were so fed up they refused to refer me to anyone. They even posted a scathing review online.

But the biggest hit wasn't my reputation—it was my finances. That job ended up costing me $8,000 out of pocket, money I didn't have to lose. And the kicker? I didn't even know how bad it was until weeks later, when my bookkeeper—a part-time one I'd hired through a friend—sent me an email asking if I'd forgotten to send her some receipts. Turns out, I wasn't just bad at tracking expenses—I was completely flying blind. I was signing checks and approving purchases without any clue where the business stood financially.

These weren't isolated incidents. The more I look back, the more I see how the small, day-to-day oversights snowballed into something bigger. Take my crew, for example. They were hard workers, but I didn't always have the right people in the right roles. I had one guy I'd hired because he was cheap, but his mistakes on-site cost me triple what I saved on his hourly rate. And then there was the time I lost a bid on a project I really wanted because I'd priced it so low, the client assumed there was no way we could do quality work. At the time, I thought I was "being competitive." Now I know I was just desperate.

What I didn't understand then—and what took me years to realize—is how deeply these failures affected me. It wasn't just about the money or the reputation; it was about how much of myself I had tied to this business. This wasn't just my job—it was part of my *identity*. So, when things started falling apart, it felt like I was falling apart *with* them.

There were nights I couldn't sleep, lying in bed with my mind racing over every mistake. I'd replay conversations with angry clients, mentally rewriting them to go differently. I'd think about my crew and the families who depended on those paychecks. And worst of all, I'd think about my own family—the wife and kids who were counting on me to make this work.

But no matter how hard I worked, it felt like I was running in quicksand. Every step forward was swallowed by another problem. I didn't know how to fix it, but I also didn't know how to admit that I couldn't. Instead, I buried myself in more work, thinking if I just pushed harder, I could dig my way out. Spoiler alert: *that's not how it works.*

It all came to a head one Friday afternoon. Payroll was due once more, and I didn't have enough in the account to cover it. I spent the morning on the phone, trying to get payments from clients who were late, but most of them had valid reasons for holding off. One guy said his bank was closed for a holiday. Another said he was waiting on a draw from his lender. A couple just didn't answer the phone.

By noon, it was clear: I couldn't make payroll. I had to face my crew and tell them the checks would be late. I'll never forget the look on their faces. Disappointment. Frustration. A couple of them didn't even bother to hide their anger. One guy, who'd been with me since the beginning, shook his head and said, "I can't do this anymore." He walked out, and three others followed him.

That was it. The dam had finally burst. I stood there in the middle of the job site, staring at the ground, feeling completely hollow. For years, I'd been telling myself I could fix things if I just worked harder, but at that moment, I knew (and understood) the truth: *the business was broken, and so was I.*

For weeks after, I avoided phone calls from vendors and clients. I just didn't have answers for them, and I didn't want to face their disappointment. I felt like a failure, not just as a business owner, but as a husband, a father, and a leader.

But in the midst of that failure, clarity began to grow. I realized that this wasn't just about bad circumstances or tough breaks. I had made choices—choices that led me *here.* I'd underbid jobs because I was afraid of losing work. I'd hired the wrong people because I wanted to save money. I'd ignored my finances because I didn't know where to start, and I was too proud to ask for help.

Admitting those things wasn't easy, but it was certainly necessary. I didn't just need to fix my business—I needed to fix the way I *thought* about running a business.

It was around this time that I heard about Timothy. A mutual acquaintance mentioned him and his consulting services during a conversation about my situation, describing him as "the guy who tells construction business owners what they don't want to hear—but need to." At first, I wasn't sure I could handle more hard truths. I felt like I'd already been hit with enough of them. But the more I thought about it, the more I realized I didn't have much left to lose.

When I finally sat down with Timothy, I'll admit, I was skeptical. He didn't sugarcoat anything. "You've been in business for years without a plan," he said. "That's like building a house without a set of blueprints. You have no idea if you're building it right." His words stung, but I knew he was right. What surprised me, though, was the relief I felt hearing them. For the first time in a long time, I didn't feel like I was carrying the weight of my mistakes alone.

"You can rebuild," he said. "But you have to start with a blueprint. And this time, you have to stick to it."

Chapter 2

The Advisor

I didn't book my meeting with Timothy right away.

I stared at his Calendly link. The subcontractor's words—"He helps contractors get their stuff together"—stuck with me, but so did my pride. I wasn't ready to admit, even to myself, just how badly I needed help. The idea of sitting in a virtual meeting, laying out the wreckage of my business, and letting them pick it apart? It made my stomach turn. I told myself I just needed more time, that I could figure things out on my own if I worked harder or hustled a little more. After all, I'd built things with my hands my whole life. Surely I could rebuild my business the same way.

But deep down, I knew I was out of my depth. No amount of grit or long hours was going to fix the mess I'd made.

The day I finally scheduled my appointment with Timothy was a low point. I'd just finished another argument with my wife about money—specifically, the lack of it. She wanted to know how we were going to pay for our bills, and I didn't have an answer. Sitting there at the kitchen table, staring at the pile of bills I couldn't pay, I felt like I was failing everyone around me. That's when I remembered the subcontractor's words.

The keyboard felt foreign as I clicked the link for our appointment. Part of me hoped he wouldn't pick up. But he did—and right on time.

"Timothy Wingate Jr.," he said, his tone clipped and professional, his smile one I'd imagine is often complimented for its charm. I could hear papers shuffling in the background.

"Uh, hi," I stammered. "I'm not sure if you remember me, but a subcontractor we both know said I should book a meeting with you. He said you help contractors—"

"Get their stuff together?" Timothy finished for me.

"Yeah," I said, feeling both exposed and oddly relieved that he knew exactly what I was trying to say.

"Let's set a meeting," he said. "Tuesday at 2. I'll send you a link via email."

That was it. No small talk, no warm introductions. Just a direct invitation to confront the mess I'd been avoiding.

***

Timothy didn't waste any time during that discovery meeting.

I sat in my office, nervously fidgeting with a pen, before he asked me to explain my business. Not the kind of surface-level explanation I'd rehearsed, but the real story. "Do you have residential or commercial contracts? Perhaps both? What's your accounting process? Do you know if all your jobs are profitable?"

I fumbled through an answer, trying to sound like I had it all under control. "Both," I said, answering his first question. "I don't have an accounting process documented. I just check my bank account every day." He waited for me to answer his third question. "I believe most of my jobs are profitable. I've been in business for 10 years."

Timothy let me finish, then leaned back in his chair through the screen, studying me with the kind of expression you'd expect from a building inspector looking at a foundation that looks like it's not leveled.

"All right," he said. "Let's get real. Why is your business failing?"

The question hit me like a gut punch. For a second, I just sat there, caught off guard by the bluntness of it. Then, slowly, I started talking. I told him about the missed deadlines, the unpaid bills, the over-budget jobs, and the payroll I couldn't cover. I even mentioned the kitchen remodel that had turned into a financial disaster. As I spoke, I could feel the weight of my failures pressing down on me, but I couldn't stop.

Timothy didn't interrupt. He just listened, occasionally jotting down notes. When I finally finished, he glanced at his notepad and said, "Okay. Let me tell you what I'm seeing here."

He broke it down like a forensic investigator analyzing a crime scene.

"First of all, you're not tracking your numbers," he said. "You don't know your job profit margins, you're not job costing your projects, and you're not using the best accounting method for construction. That's why you're scrambling to pay bills at the end of every month—you don't know what's coming in or going out."

I nodded silently, feeling both embarrassed and validated.

"Second," he continued, "you're overextending yourself. You're not estimating your jobs properly. That's why you're running into so many change orders and unexpected costs. You didn't realize how quickly this project would get out of the original scope of work."

That one stung. He wasn't wrong.

"And third," he said, "you're trying to do too much yourself. You're not delegating, you're not building a team, and you're not putting systems in place to keep things running smoothly. You're the bottleneck, and it's killing your business."

He leaned back and looked at me. "You've been running this company like it's a hustle, not a business. And if you keep doing that, you'll end up right back where you started."

I'd expected Timothy to ease into things, maybe start with some generic advice about hard work or perseverance. Instead, he went straight for the jugular. "You're treating your business like a paycheck, not a company," he said. "You're focused on keeping your head above water, but you don't even know how deep the water is."

He pulled out a sheet of paper with a few notes he'd scribbled while I was talking. "Let's start with your finances," he said. "Are you able to figure the profit margins for your last three jobs?"

I didn't answer right away, partly because I didn't want to admit I had no idea. When I finally shook my head, he just nodded, like he'd expected as much. "That's problem number one," he said. "You can't fix what you're not measuring. And right now, you're not measuring anything."

He went on to list blind spot after blind spot: I wasn't tracking job costs. I wasn't paying myself properly. I didn't have a system for estimating or bidding. I couldn't compute my quarterly estimated tax payments. The list went on, each critique hitting harder than the last. But the thing that stuck with me the most was when he said, "You've been in business for ten years, but you've been running it like it's year one."

That one stung. I wanted to argue, to defend myself, but I couldn't. He was right. I'd been so busy trying to keep things afloat that I hadn't taken the time to step back and actually run the business.

Hearing Timothy lay out my blind spots so clearly was like watching a demolition crew tear down a building I'd spent years constructing. As much as I wanted to defend myself—to argue that I'd done the best I could with what I had—I couldn't. Everything he said was true.

And yet, instead of feeling defeated, I felt... relieved. For the first time in years, someone was giving me clarity. It wasn't sugarcoated or watered down—it was raw, honest, and exactly what I needed. He wasn't pointing out my failures to tear me down—he was showing me what needed to change so I could rebuild.

"You're not the first contractor to be in this situation," he said at one point. "And you won't be the last. But the ones who succeed are the ones who are willing to face the hard truths and do the work to fix them. Are you willing to do that?"

I nodded. I didn't trust myself to speak, but I nodded.

The funny thing about Timothy was that, for all his bluntness, he didn't come off as judgmental. He wasn't sitting there, shaking his head at me like I was some lost cause. He was just... honest. Honest in a way I hadn't experienced before. And as hard as it was to hear, there was something oddly reassuring about it. He wasn't sugarcoating anything, but he also wasn't telling me anything I couldn't fix.

At one point, he said, "Look, this isn't rocket science. You don't need an MBA to run a successful construction company. But you do need a plan. And right now, you don't have one."

That was the first time in a long time I felt hope. He didn't say it outright, but the implication was clear: I could turn this around. It wasn't going to be easy, but it was possible.

Timothy laid out the basics of what I needed to do. "First, we're going to figure out your numbers. Every business's financials tells a story, and that story is always revealed through the numbers. If you're not looking at them, you're flying blind." He gave me homework: gather my bank statements, credit card statements, and any tax returns for the last three years, both business and personal. Then he added, "And while you're at it, think about what you actually want out of this business. Not what you think you're supposed to want—what you *actually* want."

That part caught me off guard. I'd spent so much time trying to survive that I hadn't thought about what success even looked like for me. Did I want a big company doing $25 million in revenue, offering benefits like health insurance and a 401(k) plan? Or did I just want something small, steady, and manageable? I didn't have an answer, but for the first time, I realized it was a question worth asking.

By the end of the meeting, Timothy had laid out a roadmap that felt both overwhelming and strangely achievable.

"Step three," he said, "is building systems. Right now, everything's in your head. That needs to change. We're going to create processes for estimating, job costing, scheduling, and everything else, so you're not constantly putting out fires."

By the time he finished, I had a to-do list longer than any I'd ever seen. But for the first time in months, I didn't feel hopeless.

After the Zoom call ended, I realized something else: *I didn't have to do this alone anymore.*

CHAPTER 3

WHAT DO YOU REALLY WANT?

"What do you really want?" he asked again during one of our sessions, leaning forward with that no-nonsense glare that cut right through the clutter of my excuses. I'd been living on autopilot for so long—chasing contracts, scrambling for cash, juggling endless projects—that I'd never paused to ask myself that simple question. But there I was, in the middle of another conversation with a man who wasn't afraid to call me out, when I realized I'd been measuring my life in dollars and deadlines, not in moments that mattered.

I walked out of my office that day feeling both deflated and oddly hopeful after our Zoom call. The buzz of the construction site, the clanging of metal, the resonant screech of machinery—all of it faded into a distant background noise as I wrestled with the question. I had always assumed that success was about scaling up: more projects, bigger contracts, a fatter bottom line. But Timothy's challenge forced me to confront a truth I'd long avoided. I wasn't sure I could even articulate what I truly wanted beyond the endless grind.

That night, alone in my small office cluttered with blueprints and overdue invoices, I sat down at my battered desk and opened a fresh notebook. I didn't have any grand plan in mind—just a desperate need to make sense of the chaos inside me. I scribbled down thoughts as they came, without worrying about neatness or business jargon. I wrote about the afternoons before the bank closed that I spent staring blankly at a phone screen waiting for payments that never came, about the mornings I'd wake up with a pit in my stomach thinking about the next crisis. But in between those grim thoughts, small memories began to surface—glimpses of a time when I believed in something bigger.

I remembered a day on a job site years ago when we were renovating an old community center. It wasn't a big, glamorous project, and the money wasn't great, but the impact we had was undeniable. I recalled how the local kids had laughed and played in a space that suddenly felt welcoming, how the principal's eyes had lit up when he thanked me for giving the building a new lease on life. That moment had stirred something inside me, a long-forgotten sense of purpose that wasn't tied to the next invoice or profit margin.

I put down my pen and leaned back in my creaky chair, trying to piece together a vision that felt authentic. *What did I really want?* I had spent so many years running on fumes—running to keep the lights on, to stave off the fear of failure—that I'd never taken the time to consider what I might be capable of building if I stopped chasing every emergency and started planning with intention. I thought about my family, too. I remembered the evenings I'd come home too tired to be present, the missed birthdays, and the quiet dinners eaten in separate rooms because I was too busy worrying about the next deadline. I wanted more than just a surviving business—I wanted a life where I wasn't sacrificing everything at the altar of work.

The next morning, I decided I had to talk to Timothy again. Not about numbers or systems this time, but about the heart of it all. I sent him an email to set up another Zoom call.

"Timothy," I started, "I've been thinking about what you said—the question about what I really want. I'm really trying to figure it out, but it's not as easy as I thought."

He sipped his tea, eyes thoughtful. "It never is," he replied. "That's because what you want isn't some one-size-fits-all answer. It's personal. It's *messy*. And it changes over time. But you've got to start somewhere."

I nodded, fiddling with the rim of my coffee cup. "I've always thought success was about growth—the bigger the company, the better. But lately, I'm wondering if it's more than that. Maybe it's about creating something that matters, something that doesn't drain every bit of me out." I paused, trying to articulate the jumble of emotions inside me. "I want my work to count for something beyond just paying the bills."

Timothy leaned forward. "Then what do you want it to count for? What legacy do you want to leave? Not just for the company, but for yourself and your family?"

That question stuck around long after I finished my coffee. That night, I drove home in a daze. When I finally pulled into my driveway, I sat in the car for a long while, staring at the darkened house and wondering if I'd ever see a future where I wasn't just a man overwhelmed by bills and deadlines.

Inside, the house was silent—my wife and kids already asleep. I went to the kitchen, poured myself a glass of water, and sat down at the table. In the quiet, I allowed myself to be honest: I was tired of the endless hustle. I was exhausted from the constant battle to keep everything from falling apart. I longed for a day when I could be fully present at dinner, when I could laugh without the gnawing worry about an overdue invoice. I wanted to build something that allowed me to *live*, not just survive.

That night, I took out the notebook again. This time, I wrote slowly, deliberately. I jotted down a list—not of business goals, but of personal ones: More time with my family, less stress on the job site, a crew that felt like a second family rather than a collection of COGS (Cost of Goods Sold) in a building. I even allowed myself to dream of a day when I'd wake up without a sense of impending doom—a day when the only thing on my mind was how to make the most of the time I had.

I didn't have all the answers. In fact, most of it felt confusing, like a puzzle with too many pieces scattered all over the place. But for the first time in a long time, I wasn't afraid to confront that confusion. I was ready to ask the hard questions, even if I didn't have neat answers.

Over the next few weeks, I made it a point to set aside time every morning to think. I'd simply sit with my coffee and my thoughts. I began to notice the small things: the way the sunrise changed colors, the sound of birds outside my window, the quiet sections of the morning before the day really began. These were the moments I'd been missing while buried under paperwork and endless to-do lists. Slowly, I started to make a change.

I shared these ideas with my wife one evening as we sat together in the living room. "I'm starting to see that what I've been chasing might not even be what I need," I said softly. "I want to build something that feels right. Not just something that makes money." She reached over and squeezed my hand. "I always believed there was more to it than just the business," she said. "I just want you to be happy—and if that means building a company that lets you live your life, then that's what we should aim for."

Her words hit home. For so long, I'd conflated success with survival, with keeping up appearances and meeting deadlines. But now, I realized that the real measure of success wasn't in the balance sheet; it was in the quality of life I was able to create for myself and those around me. "I'm done being on autopilot," I said.

I started involving my crew in these conversations too. It wasn't long before I discovered that many of them were equally tired of the constant pressure. During a break on a sweltering afternoon, I sat with Joe—the guy who had been with me since the early days. "You ever think about what you really want out of this?" I asked him, not as my foreman, but as a fellow human being. Joe looked at me, wiping sweat from his brow. "All I know is I want to go home without my brain feeling like it's been run over by a cement mixer," he replied, chuckling. But then, leaning in closer, he added quietly, "I'd like to see a day where we're not just working for the next paycheck. Maybe even enjoy what we do, you know?"

That simple conversation really resonated with me. The idea that a business could be more than just a relentless grind, that it could create a sense of pride, was both revolutionary and entirely necessary.

Timothy's questioning had set off a chain reaction in me. I began drafting a new mission statement for the business, one that didn't focus solely on growth and profit, but on quality, integrity, and balance. I jotted down in my notebook, almost as a promise to myself: "We build more than structures; we add to our community, we build relationships, we build a future where work enriches life, not drains it." Somehow, I began thinking that turning this ship around might actually become a real possibility, not by cutting corners or chasing after every contract, but by rethinking what success truly meant.

It certainly wasn't an easy process. There were days when the old habits would creep in, when the familiar fear of not being able to pay the bills or meet a deadline would try to drag me back into the old patterns. But now, I started to push back against those impulses. I began setting boundaries for myself—declining certain projects that didn't align with my new dream, reorganizing schedules to ensure I had time for family, and even encouraging my crew to speak up about what they needed to make their days less chaotic.

I remember one evening, not long after I'd been inspired, sitting at the edge of a nearly deserted job site. The sun was setting, and for a very brief moment, everything felt peaceful. I leaned against a stack of plywood and allowed myself to simply *be*. In that stillness, I realized that the balance I craved was something I would have to build into every aspect of my life, every decision I make. I had to be intentional about how

I spent my time, how I treated my team, and how I defined success.

It was a hard pill to swallow, realizing that for so long I'd been sacrificing parts of who I was in the name of progress. But in that painful admission, there was also a kind of liberation.

Chapter 4

Foundations of Failure

"Let's cut to the chase," Timothy said, leaning back in his chair as if he were about to unload the whole truth of my situation on me. I braced for impact, staring at the computer screen. "Tell me again—why is your business falling apart?" His tone wasn't angry; but it did feel disappointed, almost as if he cared enough to see you fail so you could learn something. And believe me, I needed to learn.

I took a deep breath, remembering all the nights I'd spent staring at a bank account that never seemed to fill up fast enough. It all started when I jumped headfirst into this venture without enough cash in the tank. I had the fire and the ambition, convinced I could run on sheer willpower and grit. I thought, "Money comes, money goes—just keep the work coming." But it doesn't work that way. I was living month-to-month, hoping for a miracle that never showed up. Every unexpected expense felt like a punch to the gut, and every day became a scramble to patch up holes in a sinking ship.

Timothy wasn't subtle about it. "You tried building on a heap of hope," he said. "Without real working capital, you're constructing your business on thin air." I couldn't argue with that. I remember those days when even a small bump in material prices sent me into a tailspin. I was constantly borrowing from future profits, and if one thing went wrong—which it always did—the whole thing would collapse.

Then there was the matter of me not even paying myself properly. I would write myself a check from the company sporadically. I wasn't thinking about putting myself on payroll. I was pouring every cent back into the company. Looking back, it was sheer madness.

I'd always figured that if I could put off paying myself, I'd have more money to reinvest. Instead, I ended up starving myself, both financially and emotionally. I was the engine of the business, yet I treated myself like an afterthought. It never occurred to me that putting myself on a proper payroll would actually offer significant tax advantages—from the ability to contribute to retirement accounts, to simplifying my tax reporting, to creating a more accurate picture of the business's true operating costs. I was so focused on keeping every dollar in the business that I missed how a regular salary could benefit both my personal finances and the company's long-term health. It's like I was running a marathon and never bothered to water down the side of the track for myself. Timothy's words still echo in my head: "How can the company grow if you're taking all the profits through distributions?"

I remember one particular day—an especially rough one—when I realized just how deep I was in over my head. It was a drizzly Tuesday, and I'd just finished reworking the numbers after another disastrous week. The project I'd been so proud of turned out to be a money pit, and I couldn't even figure out how to cover the basics, let alone take a cut for myself. I sat there in my tiny office, staring blankly at the spreadsheets, feeling the pressure of my own stubborn pride. I had been so afraid to admit I was failing that I buried myself in more work, trying to fix everything on the fly. But trying to patch up a collapsing roof with duct tape never ends well.

And then there was my approach to hiring. I always thought that saving a few bucks by hiring the cheapest hands was smart business. "It's just cutting costs," I'd tell myself, convincing myself that a little extra oversight could fix any mistake. But every time I brought in someone unskilled, the errors piled up. I hired men who didn't know the difference between a proper foundation and a hastily poured slab. I watched in dismay as their mistakes cost us rework, delays, and a lot of angry phone calls from clients. I still see the memory of one job—a remodel that should have been a simple fix—turn into a never-ending mess of redos and repairs because someone had cut corners to save a buck. The irony is brutal: trying to save money on labor ended up costing me far more in lost time and wasted resources.

Timothy was brutally honest about that, too. "Your cheap labor isn't cheap—it's costing you in every way possible," he said one afternoon, shaking his head as he flipped through the notes he'd taken during our meetings. "You're building a house of cards, and the slightest gust of wind will send it crashing down." His words stung, but they were true. I'd been so caught up in chasing lower costs that I ignored the obvious truth: quality work, like quality people, isn't free.

Then there was the mess I made of my financial systems. I had no real system at all—just a chaotic jumble of spreadsheets, whiteboard, and a general "wing it" attitude. I didn't know where the money was going because I wasn't tracking it properly. I was too busy handling crises to keep up with the numbers. I remember that fateful email from my part-time bookkeeper, asking for receipts that I'd carelessly stuffed into a truck console. It was a minor sign at first, but soon I realized that I was basically running blind. Every time I signed a check or approved a purchase, I was doing so without a clear picture of my finances. It was reckless, and it put the entire business at risk.

On top of that, I'd completely sidestepped proper tax planning. Taxes were the boogeyman in the back of my mind—a problem I'd always intended to tackle "when things got better." But things never got better, and before I knew it, I was scrambling every quarter to set aside money I didn't even have. The stress was suffocating, and it took a toll not just on my bank account but on my peace of mind.

Loans were another can of worms I'd opened without a plan. I'd taken on debt like it was a lifeline, convinced that I could pay it off later when the projects rolled in. Instead, I found myself caught in a vicious cycle of borrowing to cover previous mistakes. Every month, when the statements arrived, I felt like I was staring at the very blueprint of my failure.

And then there was my cavalier approach to subcontractors. In my desperate bid to cut costs, I'd often hired men who weren't insured—men who gave me low bids to do the work but brought with them a load of risk. I remember one project quite vividly: we had hired a subcontractor without proper insurance, and a mishap on the site not only delayed the work but also left us facing a potential liability that threatened to ruin us. I was so caught up in chasing a bargain that I'd forgotten the value of protection. Timothy's words on this were like another punch to the gut. "Every uninsured subcontractor is a gamble," he told me. "And you're not in the business of gambling."

Sitting there, with Timothy's assessments cutting through my defenses, I couldn't help but feel like I was staring at the wreckage of a life built on mistakes. The lack of working capital meant I was always scrambling; the failure to pay myself properly meant I was undervaluing my own worth; hiring unskilled workers led to costly errors; and my financial systems were so disorganized that I was essentially blindfolded when it came to managing my business.

I could see it all now, laid out in harsh, undeniable clarity. I was the sum of every miscalculation, every rash decision, every time I'd chosen a shortcut over a solid method. And while that realization stung, it also sparked something inside me. I finally understood that if I was ever going to salvage what remained of my business, I needed to start from scratch. I needed to rebuild.

Timothy's approach wasn't to beat me down, but to force me to see the truth. "You've been constructing your business on what I'd call a 'foundation of excuses,'" he said. "It's time to tear it all down and rebuild with some real discipline. Learn from every screw that's gone loose, every mistake that cost you dearly. There's no magic fix here—only hard work and honest reckoning."

I began to spend long nights not just worrying about the next project, but dissecting every decision that had led me to this point. I revisited old job files, re-read client complaints, and looked at the figures with brutal honesty. I saw the patterns—the same mistakes cropping up over and over, like a broken record I couldn't stop playing.

So, I planned to start making changes—small shifts that would be anything but easy. First, I took a long, hard look at my finances. I was going to ditch the old, haphazard system and invest in proper accounting software. I told myself I'd dedicate hours to learning how to track every dollar, no matter how tedious it felt. I'd set up monthly reviews and even start scheduling meetings with a strategic advisor who specialized in construction businesses. I knew it wasn't glamorous work, but it was necessary. I had to know exactly where I stood if I was ever going to steer this ship out of troubled waters.

Next, with Timothy's help, I started to rethink my hiring strategy. I made the hard decision to stop cutting corners on labor costs. I would reach out to experienced workers, even if it meant paying a bit more. I would start a training program to ensure that every new hire understood not just how to do the work, but why quality mattered.

I also planned to overhaul my approach to subcontractors. Gone were the days of chasing the cheapest bid and losing cashflow because of their demand to be paid weekly. Every subcontractor I would engage with now had to meet a strict set of standards, including submitting a detailed scope of work, proper insurance, and submitting their invoices on time to receive payment. I'd spend time on the phone, scrutinizing references, and even visiting some of their previous job sites to ensure that their work was as solid as I needed it to be. It was going to be a painstaking process, but it was one I no longer saw as optional.

Then it would be time for the personal transformation—the realization that I had to value myself as much as I valued the business. I would finally start paying myself a proper salary through a payroll provider. If I was going to expect my crew to show up and give their best every day, I needed to lead by example. "Taking care of yourself shouldn't be seen as a luxury. It's a necessity," Timothy said. After all, I couldn't pour from an empty cup, no matter how many projects I had lined up.

And taxes? I'd certainly start taking that seriously, too. Timothy helped to demystify the complicated world of tax planning for me. I finally learned about deductions, credits, and the importance of staying ahead of quarterly deadlines. It was a slow process, but everything I was learning made the looming specter of tax season just a little less terrifying.

Through all of these changes, Timothy was going to be there to remind me that I was not destined to repeat my past mistakes. "Keep at it," he'd say.

CHAPTER 5

BUILDING BLOCKS OF A PLAN

"So, you've been in business for 10 years doing things the wrong way," Timothy said, eyes locked on mine. I gulped. "It's not going to be fixed in 10 months. Now you need to implement a plan. I know I keep saying it, but you do. A *real* plan. Are you ready for the long haul?"

I leaned back in my chair, absorbing his challenge without a hint of theatrics. I'd been expecting another lecture on my past mistakes, but instead, Timothy was outlining the way *forward*. There was no sugar-coating here. I was done with just patching up the issues as they came. It was time to stop firefighting and start building something that could actually stand on its own.

Timothy pulled out a notepad and scribbled down a few key questions. "First off," he said, "what do you want this business to be? A small $500,000 company or a $25 million company? Residential or commercial? Or are you thinking about diversifying? Because without a clear vision, even the best strategies won't work." He looked at me as if expecting an answer I wasn't prepared to give.

I ran through the possibilities in my head. For years, I'd just taken whatever work came my way, never stopping to consider what the end game really was. Was I content with being a local contractor, slinging bids and barely scraping by? Or was I ready to build something that could eventually handle better, more profitable projects? The questions weren't easy, but they were necessary. Timothy's challenge forced me to confront the simple truth: I needed to decide what I was aiming for.

"We need a vision," Timothy continued. "Without it, you're just drifting. And in construction, drifting means you'll end up with a mix of half-baked projects that don't add up to a coherent business. You need to define your identity—what kind of projects you take, what your standards are, even what your company stands for."

I listened, nodding slowly. I wasn't used to having someone ask me the hard questions about the future. Usually, I was too busy putting out fires to think about where I was headed. But here was an opportunity to change that course.

Timothy laid out the first step: establishing a clear business identity. "It's not enough to just show up and do the work," he said. "You need to know who you are in this market. Are you the contractor who does quality renovations? Are you the one who's best at commercial builds? Or do you specialize in something else entirely? Define it, own it, and then build your reputation around that."

Next came the issue of systems. "A strong business needs solid systems," he said, tapping his notepad. "That means implementing reliable accounting systems, tracking every dollar that comes in and goes out. You need to know your profit margins, your job costs—every single number. And you need to implement the right accounting method to qualify for future opportunities like bonding and larger lines of credit. Without this implementation, it will be hard for you to track multiple projects and manage bigger projects."

"I've gotten started, but I definitely need your help," I said, hoping to sound humorous.

"It's going to be tedious," he warned. "But if you want to build a company that can grow, you have to put in the work now."

Timothy's tone was matter-of-fact. There was no dramatic pause or sentimental look back at all the failures I'd endured. He wasn't dwelling on the past—he was focused on what needed to be done today to ensure tomorrow wasn't just a repeat of my previous mistakes.

He continued by outlining a few critical milestones. "Bonding is one of those milestones that'll open up more opportunities for you," he explained. "Without proper bonding, you're stuck in a small pool of projects. But bonding requires experience with projects you're seeking bonding for, good accounting records, and a good business and personal credit history. That means you need to fix what's broken *now* before you can even think about scaling."

I listened as he methodically went through each step. "You have to fix your current business," he said bluntly, "and that means being ruthless with your processes. Don't just put out fires—set up systems so fires don't start in the first place."

The conversation eventually shifted to defining concrete, *long-term* goals. Timothy asked pointed questions: "Do you want to be known as the contractor who never misses a deadline, who always delivers quality work? Or do you want to be the guy who's always struggling just to keep up?"

I spent the next few hours in that tiny office, hammering out details with Timothy over a Zoom call. We discussed actionable steps: setting up a formal accounting system, reworking the hiring process to focus on skilled labor, creating a business plan that clearly defined the type of projects we'd focus on, and establishing measurable benchmarks for progress.

I left our call that day with a notebook full of action items and a mind buzzing with possibilities. For the first time in years, I wasn't just thinking about survival. I was high on the idea that growth was attainable. I had a clear question to answer: *What do I want this business to be?* The answer was still a mystery to me.

That day, I tore through the backlog of paperwork. I set up a meeting with my core team, laying out the new plan as plainly as I could. There was no need for a grand speech. I simply explained that from now on, things were going to change. We were going to start keeping better track of our numbers, re-evaluate every project with a critical eye, and begin focusing on the type of work that aligned with our new vision. I didn't sugarcoat the fact that it was going to be a long, tough road—one that required discipline, hard work, and, most importantly, a willingness to change the way we'd always done things.

One of the first changes was overhauling our accounting system. I pulled out every receipt, invoice, and bank statement from the past few years. I installed a new accounting software. Slowly, the numbers began to make sense. I could see where we'd been bleeding money, which projects were profitable, and which ones were nothing more than money pits.

Simultaneously, I re-evaluated our hiring practices. I made the difficult decision to let go of a few workers who didn't meet the standards we needed for the new direction. It wasn't personal. I knew that quality work was non-negotiable if we were going to move forward. I began recruiting skilled laborers, people who not only knew their craft but also understood the importance of precision and reliability. I even started a training program to bring everyone up to the same level of expertise.

We also set out to redefine our brand. I worked on a simple, clear business identity that could be communicated both to potential clients and to our team. We decided to focus on quality and reliability over sheer volume. That meant being selective about the projects we took on and ensuring that every job was executed to the highest standard. There were no (and would be no) shortcuts. Clients would know that when they hired us, they were investing in a business that had its act together.

Another crucial aspect was planning for bonding. We started laying the groundwork for bonding applications by cleaning up our accounting records and demonstrating a steady track record of completed projects. It was like I could feel Timothy pushing me forward in the back of my mind. "Keep at it."

Every day, I reviewed the plan with a critical eye. I didn't allow myself to get complacent or assume that just because we'd made some changes, the job was done. The reality was that the transformation would be gradual. Even still, there were quiet days when the old, thrown-out habits threatened to creep back in—when the temptation to take on a project simply because it was available was hard to resist. But each time I felt that pull, I'd refer back to the clear questions Timothy had laid out for me. *Was this project going to help build the kind of business I envisioned? Did it align with our new identity?*

One afternoon, a few months into this new approach, I was on a job site discussing a project with my new foreman. As we reviewed the day's schedule, he said, "It's like you've turned the whole operation around. I've never seen things run this tight." I didn't grin like I used to; instead, I simply nodded.

Chapter 6

A Blueprint for the Who

I'd reached a point where I didn't want to hear any more platitudes about perseverance or how "everyone makes mistakes." I understood that already; it was the reason I'd spent so many nights staring at the ceiling, wondering how on earth the business had veered so far off course. It wasn't just about missing deadlines or juggling a string of late payments anymore. It was about finally admitting that I was treading water because the people I surrounded myself with couldn't—or wouldn't—help me swim. For too long, I'd prioritized simply filling open slots over carefully selecting the right individuals. Timothy, who'd seen plenty of contractors tangle themselves in the same mess, was determined to make sure I understood how critical it was to put quality at the heart of every hiring decision.

He'd told me weeks earlier, "You have to make sure you have the right people in the right seat on the bus. You can't implement a grand plan if your crew can't handle it." At the time, I'd nodded, filing the phrase away with all the other advice I'd gotten—advice I half-listened to while I was desperately trying to keep the company afloat. But everything began to hit differently once I'd accepted that my biggest obstacles weren't the market or the economy or my track record. The biggest obstacles were the folks I'd brought on board without vetting their work ethic or their alignment with my goals. I'd hired because of convenience or short-term cost savings. I'd hired because I was desperate, or because someone else said they were "good enough." And each time I compromised, the real price I paid went well beyond a paycheck.

On the morning Timothy and I tackled the topic head-on, I was sitting in my office with a notebook already half-filled with regrets. I'd written down the names of people I'd hired, next to the projects I'd assigned them to. I'd also noted the problems that came up because of these hires: rework that delayed entire schedules, unhappy clients who had zero faith in our ability to deliver, friction on-site that made every day feel like a slog. Timothy gave the list a quick glance through the webcam and pressed his lips together in a way that told me he wasn't surprised. He'd heard these stories a hundred times from other contractors, but that didn't make my situation any less urgent.

"That foreman you hired," Timothy said, pointing to the first name on the list, "why did you pick him? Was it purely because you thought you could pay him less?" I admitted that was the reason. He was an experienced worker on paper—or so he had claimed—though the moment I put him in charge of a team, the cracks started showing. He either lacked the basic leadership skills to keep people motivated, or he didn't care enough to implement any meaningful structure. I had stepped in multiple times to do his job for him, which meant I was barely doing my own job as the owner. My time was spent chasing down smaller tasks and smoothing over issues his negligence caused. If I had tallied up the money lost in mistakes, wasted hours, and late completions, I would have realized that my so-called "bargain hire" cost more than a qualified manager would have in the first place.

Timothy folded his arms and stared at me through the screen for a moment. "Let's be crystal clear. You're not running a charity or a social club. It's a business. Don't hire people out of pity or just because you need a warm body. That's not fair to you or the rest of the team. Your entire crew is forced to compensate for someone who's underperforming. That's how resentment builds. And trust me, once that sets in, productivity and morale take a nosedive. You need to do better."

I didn't argue. I'd spent enough hours on job sites watching crew members roll their eyes behind a foreman's back or ignore a new guy who didn't seem to care about quality. Those attitudes seeped into everything. If the foreman couldn't coordinate tasks properly, people lost faith, and corners inevitably got cut. The ripple effect made it harder for me to land new projects, because word travels fast when you develop a reputation for disorganized work. In construction, referrals are gold, and I'd been squandering them by failing to staff projects with people who cared.

Timothy's approach from the start was tough but fair. He was just making sure I understood that if I kept ignoring these cracks in my workforce, the entire operation would collapse. He told me a story about a contractor he once advised who tried to expand too fast without addressing fundamental hiring gaps. "That guy was taking on big commercial builds but hired a bunch of underqualified laborers and half-committed supervisors," Timothy said. "He thought sheer volume of workers would cover for a lack of skill. It didn't. The rework alone nearly bankrupted him." I caught myself nodding along because I was on the same path, just at a slower pace.

We spent a while dissecting different roles in my current lineup. I had a few shining stars—people who worked their tails off and actually improved the workflow whenever they showed up. But those were the exceptions. The rest of the team was a mix of untested beginners, jaded professionals, and folks who only half-bought into the idea of producing quality craftsmanship on a consistent basis. When Timothy asked me why I'd hired each person, my answers felt absurd the moment I said them out loud. One was a cousin's referral who needed a job fast, so I jumped at the chance to bring him on board. Another was a friend-of-a-friend who claimed he could estimate better than anyone else, but I never bothered to verify that skill in any formal way. Once I got in the habit of "hire fast, hope for the best," it was almost impossible to break out of it. And as we sat there, I realized that my failure to screen people properly was the root cause of most of the chaos in my business.

Timothy gave me a look, subtly trying to remind me of the phrase he'd told me to write in my notebook: "You have to make sure you have the right people in the right seat on the bus." We'd talked about this mantra before, but now I felt the gravity of it sinking in. "You're so caught up in all the tasks that need doing," he said, "and I get it—you're used to wearing a dozen hats. But none of that matters if the people under those hats can't do the job right. Stop focusing on tasks, start focusing on who is actually performing them." He pointed out that I'd taken steps to fix other aspects of the business: tightening up my accounting, clarifying my overall vision, trying to keep the schedule realistic. Those were all good moves, but if the people implementing those moves didn't align with the company's standards, we'd keep fighting the same battles.

He leaned forward in his chair, still staring into his webcam. "It's time to raise your standards. If you're not willing to take a hard look at who's on your payroll, you're wasting your time with everything else." I sat there, absorbing the reprimand, but also feeling oddly energized. I wanted to do better, not just for the sake of the numbers, but because I was tired of the drama. I didn't need any more days wasted on trying to figure out why so-and-so showed up late or left a job site half-finished. I wanted a culture of people who took pride in their work and felt responsible for the final product. That ambition, Timothy said, starts with me.

I thought back to the times I'd gotten pushback from the crew. Whenever I tried to implement a new procedure or scheduling system, certain folks would shrug and say, "That's not how we did it on the last job," or "I've been doing this for twenty years; I don't need new-fangled methods." In many of those situations, I'd caved. I was afraid if I pushed too hard, they'd walk, and I'd be left even more short-staffed than before. But Timothy helped me see that if they walked, maybe that wouldn't be such a bad thing. Clinging to people who refused to evolve was costing me far more than I realized. "You're paying for resistance," Timothy said. "They might clock in, but if they're not aligned, they're eroding your culture from the inside."

There was a particular project manager, Garrett, who popped into my mind the second Timothy said that. Garrett was a good talker and had convinced me early on that he was capable of juggling multiple builds. But after a few weeks, it was clear he operated with zero accountability. If a sub missed a deadline, Garrett blamed the sub. If materials got delayed, he blamed the supplier. He never once owned up to the fact that half the time, he was late ordering those materials or neglected to check the sub's references. When I brought up these issues, he'd wave them away or change the subject. I put up with it because I thought I needed him, that I'd never find someone with his "experience." But all the experience in the world is worthless if you can't manage the responsibilities that come with it. Timothy suggested that maybe it was time to let Garrett go, or at the very least, put him on a performance improvement plan. "No more free passes," Timothy said. "You want a culture of excellence, you have to promote excellence."

That night, I actually called Garrett into my office. I'd made a list of all the tasks he'd fumbled in the last month. It was longer than I'd hoped. I laid it out calmly, explaining that this wasn't about pointing fingers but about clarifying expectations. I told him the mistakes couldn't continue, that we needed accountability on every step of the process, and that I'd be creating a more structured system for him to follow.

Instead of taking it as constructive feedback, he deflected. He said he'd been "stretched too thin" by the field crews and that I should hire more assistants. He had a reason for every shortcoming, and none of them involved him taking responsibility. By the end of that meeting, I knew we'd hit a wall. If he couldn't own his role in the chaos, I couldn't keep him on as a project manager.

I talked it over with Timothy during our next Zoom call, feeling a bit of that old sense of dread about losing a staff member who filled an important slot. "Look," Timothy told me, "yes, losing a project manager hurts short-term. But you're losing money on him anyway if he's failing to deliver. Better to have a temporary gap than let someone anchor the entire operation." That phrase—anchor the entire operation—stuck with me. How many times had I let the wrong hire anchor me in place, stalling momentum because I was too cautious to let them go?

We also discussed the future roles I'd need to fill if I was going to turn this company around. Timothy wanted me to think carefully about each position before I wrote a single job posting. "You've got to know exactly what you want," he said, "not just in terms of skill, but in terms of attitude and alignment. If you skip that step, you'll end up with another round of unmotivated hires who have no clue why they're here or what success looks like." I took his words to heart and started listing out non-negotiables for every job role, from field laborers to office staff.

Timothy, never one to be satisfied with half measures, also encouraged me to revise how I conducted interviews. "Try to get a sense of who they are under pressure," he advised. "Construction can be a grind. You need people who don't fold the moment something goes off-schedule." We talked about setting up scenario-based questions and even hands-on tasks for certain roles. If someone claimed to be a top-notch carpenter, I wanted to see them measure a space and mark cuts quickly, accurately, and confidently. If they said they could read blueprints, I'd hand them a simple plan and ask them what the biggest red flag might be in that design. By making the interview process more demanding, I'd weed out the people who were hoping to bluff their way in.

In one of our sessions, Timothy shared a conversation he'd had with another contractor who'd made a breakthrough by inviting a prospective project manager to shadow a job for half a day before finalizing the hire. It gave everyone a chance to see if there was a natural fit. The candidate got to feel the pace of the crew and the company vibe, and the boss got to see if the candidate melted under real-world stress. Timothy thought the same approach could work for me, especially since my biggest weakness was hiring in a rush and hoping for the best. With a half-day shadow, I wouldn't just hear a candidate's brag sheet—I'd watch them in action. When I tried it out, I was amazed at how quickly someone's real character showed under the demands of a busy site.

Of course, none of this was a quick fix. We had ongoing projects that needed bodies on site, and every day that I spent crafting a more rigorous hiring process was another day I was short-staffed. But Timothy's logic grounded me. "Better to be short a couple of people than to fill those slots with folks who can't do the job or won't respect the company's direction," he said. I couldn't deny the truth of that. If I kept patching holes with subpar hires, I'd be stuck in the same endless cycle of rework and disappointment.

As we refined our plan, Timothy brought up the point that once I started bringing in better-qualified folks, I'd also have to pay them what they were worth. "If you're going to demand excellence, you should be prepared to reward it," he said. That didn't necessarily mean overpaying, but it did mean being fair and transparent. The best workers out there know what they bring to the table. If I wasn't willing to meet them halfway, they'd find another contractor who would. This was especially important for roles where skill and experience make all the difference, like a lead carpenter or a site supervisor who can manage a crew of ten with minimal drama. "You can't nickel-and-dime quality," Timothy reminded me. "Every time you try, you end up paying double for mistakes."

As the weeks rolled on, I started seeing glimmers of positive change. A few people who didn't appreciate the new, more structured environment drifted away on their own. At first, I worried about the gaps they left, but something interesting happened. The folks who remained stepped up their game. A foreman who used to wait for me to make every call began handling small crises on-site without needing my permission. The office manager who previously needed a push to stay on top of phone calls took the initiative to reorganize our scheduling board. I even overheard two of our carpenters telling a new hire that if he wasn't prepared to follow the procedure for daily site cleanups, he should find somewhere else to work. The culture was beginning to shift, and it was happening because I was finally drawing a line in the sand about who got to be part of this company.

I reported all this to Timothy in our subsequent check-ins. He'd nod, a small, satisfied smile spreading across his face whenever I mentioned someone who had either stepped up or stepped out. "That's what happens when you set a standard," he said more than once. "You attract people who respect it and repel the ones who don't. It's not magic; it's simply how culture works." Hearing that over and over made me wish I'd started paying attention to culture years ago. In the early days, I'd believed that culture was some fluffy concept better suited to big corporations with HR departments, not a construction outfit working in dusty fields. But I'd seen how ignoring culture got me into trouble. The attitudes, the work ethic, the willingness to do things right the first time—that was our culture, whether I'd actively shaped it or not. And letting underperformers slide had effectively shaped it into a place where mediocrity found a home.

I also learned an important truth about leadership: the team was never going to care more about the business than I did. If I accepted sloppy work or let deadlines slide, they would too. If I didn't value my time or the clients' time, neither would they. So with every shift in hiring practices, I also had to shift my own behavior. I forced myself to be more consistent—if I said I'd show up on site at seven, I was there at six-fifty with coffee. If I told a client we'd finish by the end of the week, I pushed the team to meet that deadline unless a genuine catastrophe got in the way. And if someone missed the mark, I addressed it immediately. No more burying problems or hoping they'd fix themselves.

The change wasn't always pleasant. I had hard conversations with longtime employees who were used to the old ways. A few of them resisted, accusing me of becoming too rigid or "selling out." But I stayed firm, echoing Timothy's advice: if the business kept going the way it had been, there wouldn't be a business in another year. Sometimes it meant letting people go who'd been around a while, and that stung. But as each week passed, the results spoke for themselves. Jobs were completed closer to schedule, we had fewer client complaints, and we even saw a small uptick in word-of-mouth referrals from satisfied homeowners and developers.

Timothy, in his usual manner, refused to let me rest on small wins. "This is great progress," he told me, "but you need to keep refining. Hiring is not a one-and-done process. It's ongoing. You're always on the lookout for good talent, always measuring performance, and always weeding out folks who don't match the culture." He urged me to invest a bit more time in writing a proper employee handbook—one that reflected our evolving values and procedures. The idea felt a bit corporate for a small company, but I saw the potential. If I had clear guidelines about site safety, daily standards, communication protocols, and accountability structures, new hires would know exactly what they were signing up for from day one. And existing employees would have no excuse if they started bending the rules.

After working through the handbook drafts with Timothy, I decided to schedule a team meeting where I handed out a shortened version of it. Standing in the break room, I felt a brief wave of nerves. I wasn't sure how people would react. But I laid it out: here's what we stand for, here's what we won't tolerate, and here's how we'll reward consistency and excellence. The response was mostly positive. A couple of the more jaded guys grumbled, but as I looked around the room, I saw that the majority seemed relieved to have clarity. So many tensions on job sites stem from unwritten rules and guesswork about what's acceptable. By explaining everything upfront, I was cutting through that ambiguity. If someone decided they couldn't or wouldn't meet these standards, I made it clear they were free to find work elsewhere.

One of the best decisions I made during this period was to promote a quiet but reliable carpenter named Marcus to a sort of team lead position. Marcus had never asked for the role—he just did his job impeccably and occasionally pointed out small inefficiencies that could be fixed if we paid attention. The difference between Marcus and the old foreman was night and day. He didn't raise his voice or push blame around. He just calmly got things done, and he expected the same from others. When I saw him defusing a minor conflict on site by patiently walking both sides through the schedule, I realized he was precisely the kind of person I wanted in a leadership role. He was levelheaded, solution-oriented, and quietly ambitious. Timothy called this "promoting from within whenever it makes sense," because it rewards good behavior and fosters loyalty among the crew. Instead of bringing in someone from outside who'd have to learn our culture, I was nurturing someone who already embodied it.

That simple move—giving Marcus more responsibility—had a ripple effect. Other workers saw that competence and dedication could actually lead to advancement. They started sharpening their own skills and paying attention to detail, hoping to be the next one tapped for a leadership role. Even the small changes, like insisting that tools be cleaned and stowed correctly at the end of each day, gained traction when the team saw that I was serious about it and that their new leader wasn't cutting corners either.

Within a few months, job sites began to feel different. Instead of a group of random hires who showed up to punch the clock, it looked more like a cohesive team that took ownership. Sure, we still made mistakes—construction is never perfect, and unexpected issues always pop up—but the difference was in how the crew responded. They owned their errors, fixed them fast, and figured out how to avoid them next time. Clients were noticing, too. I had one developer say, "I've worked with you before, and this is a whole new ballgame. Your people seem genuinely engaged." That comment was worth its weight in gold because it confirmed that the culture shift wasn't just in my imagination.

All of these changes reaffirmed what Timothy had hammered into my head from the start: the individuals you hire shape your company more than any business plan or marketing strategy ever could. I began to see my role not merely as the "boss" but as a curator of talent and a protector of the culture I was building. It forced me to be more intentional with interviews, references, and how I integrated new hires into the team. The positive feedback loop—where good hires reinforce a good culture, which then attracts more good hires—was a breath of fresh air after years of feeling like I was dragging the entire company behind me, step by painful step.

Timothy wasn't about to let me get complacent, though. He insisted I keep thorough records of each employee's performance and progress, not just in a formal sense but so I could see trends early. If someone started slipping or showing signs of burnout, I needed to address it immediately, either by offering support or by reevaluating their fit. He also suggested that I consider performance-based bonuses at least twice a year to make sure they remained competitive. "Don't let a great worker slip away because you were too stingy to give them a raise," he'd say. "Replacing someone costs more in the long run than keeping a solid, trained, and motivated employee." I knew he was right. I'd experienced firsthand how expensive turnover can be, even if the person leaving wasn't top-tier in terms of skill.

I also started carving out a bit of time each week for one-on-ones with my key players. Just a quick coffee or a walk around the job site to check in. I'd ask how things were going, if they needed any resources, and whether there were any bottlenecks I wasn't aware of. Sometimes they'd open up about issues with subs or mention a new approach we might try. Other times, it was just a quick conversation that reinforced that I cared about their input. Those small gestures added up. People felt heard, and when people feel heard, they're more likely to stay invested in the job. Timothy had told me early on that "a good leader listens more than he lectures," and while it took a bit of discipline for me to do that—since I was used to being the one shouting orders—it quickly became my favorite part of the week.

The biggest shift, though, was my own mindset. I stopped looking for quick fixes or short-term solutions in hiring. I no longer believed that my labor problems would magically resolve if I just found one or two people who could do a job cheaply. Instead, I started to see every new hire as an investment that would either pay back dividends in productivity and harmony or drain my resources if they weren't a good fit. Once I made that internal pivot, the temptation to compromise on quality faded. I didn't want warm bodies anymore. I wanted the right bodies, people who would raise the bar and hold themselves accountable to it.

During a particularly detailed Zoom call about our hiring progress, Timothy seemed especially pleased with the photos I'd shared of our latest project site. We'd been discussing how the new team culture was manifesting in more organized job sites, better communication, and higher quality work.

"You know," Timothy said, leaning closer to his webcam with genuine enthusiasm, "what you're showing me here represents real progress. Your crew is actually wearing company uniforms now! That's not just about looking professional—it's about identity, about belonging to something meaningful."

I'd sent him photos of the team, all wearing matching shirts with our company logo, working in coordinated groups rather than the scattered approach we once had. The difference was visible even through digital images.

"I can see Marcus in these photos," Timothy continued, "working with those younger carpenters. That's exactly the kind of leadership development we talked about. He's training the next generation right there."

Timothy's validation meant everything. His thumbs-up, even across the digital divide, symbolized that we were finally on the right track. Our video calls had shifted from crisis management to progress reports, and I could see in his expression that he was genuinely impressed by how far we'd come.

"Remember when we first started talking about hiring?" he asked. "You were convinced your problems were about cash flow, projects, the economy—everything but the people. Now you can see the truth with your own eyes: when you put the right people in the right roles, everything else starts falling into place."

I couldn't disagree. The evidence was right there on my screen, and in every measurable aspect of our business. Better hiring had indeed led to better performance, fewer problems, and happier clients.

"Keep your eye on the ball," Timothy reminded me as our call wrapped up. "Your business will thrive or dive depending on who you put in those roles. Never forget that you set the tone. If you slack on your standards, they'll slack too. If you're serious about quality, they'll catch on."

I couldn't have said it better myself.

Chapter 7

Hiring Right the First Time

I still remember the exact moment I realized my entire hiring process was fundamentally broken. It was getting better, but it was still broken. It was a late afternoon, and I was at my desk, staring at a messy cluster of résumés and loose sheets of paper where I'd scribbled half-baked notes. I had a stress headache so fierce that the overhead lights felt like they were drilling into my skull. My phone buzzed for what must have been the tenth time that day—someone else complaining about a co-worker who didn't show up on time, or who messed up a crucial step on-site. I was ready to snap.

Bzz. Bzz. It was then that I suddenly remembered I had a Zoom call scheduled with Timothy, and I'd nearly forgotten! I entered the Zoom waiting room just in time. Timothy appeared, took one look at the chaos written all over my face, and nodded toward the pile of papers in the periphery. "So, this is how you pick who's going to build your reputation?" he asked.

I felt heat rush to my cheeks. "I'm doing the best I can," I said, hating how defensive I sounded.

He raised an eyebrow. "That's the problem," he replied. "It's not about doing your best. It's about having a system. Hiring is the most important step in building any company, and you're treating it like guesswork."

I thought back over the years to all the people I'd hired on a whim. The older carpenter who swore he'd worked on high-end remodels but eventually admitted he'd only helped his cousin build a shed once. The office administrator who froze any time the phone rang with a client complaint. The laborer who claimed he knew how to read blueprints but walked off the job site when asked to prove it. These hires had cost me money, time, and my sanity. Timothy was right: it wasn't "poor circumstances." It was me, rushing to fill gaps and praying each new person would somehow be "the one."

"You've got to stop repeating the same mistakes," Timothy told me. "Slow down and ask yourself: how can I truly figure out if someone's the right fit for my business?"

I looked at the stack of paper on my desk and admitted it—he was right. I'd rely on phone calls, half an hour of chat, maybe a glance at a reference list, and if they could start next week, I'd hand them a W-4. No wonder the results were mixed. It felt like picking lottery numbers in the dark.

The truth was, I never had a formal hiring process. If someone showed up wearing work boots and holding a half-decent résumé, I figured we'd make it work. Timothy wanted me to realize it was more than just a seat to fill or a pair of hands to hold a hammer. Every hire would either strengthen or weaken the entire operation. After years of frustration, I finally accepted that it was time to get serious about how I brought people onto the team.

A few days later, Timothy and I were on a Zoom call, hammering out a plan. He introduced me to two books he wanted me to check out: *Who* by Geoff Smart and *Hiring TKO* by Dave Anderson. I'd never heard of them. My reading list mostly consisted of building codes or vendor catalogs, but Timothy insisted these books were essential.

"These aren't just corporate management theory," he said. "They're practical guides to finding people who align with your goals, your culture, and your standards."

I frowned. "Culture?" I asked. "We're a construction outfit, not a tech startup."

He wasn't amused. "Culture matters anywhere you have more than one person working toward something bigger. You've seen how a few bad apples can drag everyone down. You need folks who live and breathe the same values you're trying to instill."

He popped open a notebook and started scribbling a few lines. "Let's say you have a candidate who claims to be a top-notch carpenter. On paper, they check every box: ten years of experience, references from two or three contractors. But do they share your vision for doing things right the first time? Do they adapt when a problem arises, or do they start blaming others? Will they respect the rest of the crew, or treat them like grunts? That's culture."

I began to see just how often I'd ignored these questions. In the past, if someone looked good on paper and could show up Monday, I'd hire them. Then I'd spend months putting out the fires they caused—or letting them slide because I felt too short-handed to rock the boat.

"I want you to take this as seriously as your finances," Timothy said. "You saw how mismanaging your money almost sank you. Hiring is no different. If you keep trusting random instincts and crossing your fingers, don't be surprised when you get random, inconsistent results."

I started reading *Who* by Geoff Smart, and I remember highlighting a line about how a rigorous hiring process might seem overkill, but it saves a business from the tremendous costs of a bad hire. My track record provided plenty of evidence for that. One employee who slacked off or made mistakes could tank a whole project. One underperforming foreman could alienate half the crew, push back deadlines, and poison the mood on site. Then there were the client relationships that soured when they realized the person I'd assigned to manage the project wasn't competent. The overhead of rework alone felt like it was gnawing at our profits every month.

When I shared these thoughts with Timothy, he nodded. "That's why I keep telling you to slow down and hire right the first time. It might take a few extra weeks to find someone who really clicks, but that's nothing compared to the months you'll lose trying to fix mistakes from a wrong hire."

Then he introduced me to a concept I'd never heard of: the KOLBE assessment. He explained that, unlike a standard personality test that claims to tell you how extroverted or agreeable you are, KOLBE focuses on how a person naturally approaches problem-solving. It measures something called "conative" abilities—basically, how you operate under stress and how you're likely to tackle real-world tasks.

"In construction," Timothy said, "stuff goes wrong all the time. Material shortages, weather delays, clients changing their minds last minute—none of this is theoretical. If your new project manager or lead carpenter freezes up when the plan derails, that's a nightmare. You need people who can adapt and think on their feet. KOLBE can give you a glimpse of that."

I was skeptical at first. Could a test really show me if someone had that spark I was looking for? But Timothy insisted I give it a try on a couple of potential hires. "You can still do interviews, check references—this isn't a silver bullet. But it's one more data point to help you avoid the warm-body syndrome you've been battling."

He also mentioned something else called the Strength Assessment by Ministry Insights. "It's less about problem-solving and more about how a person's strengths fit with the team," he explained. "Some folks thrive on details, others are big-picture thinkers. You need both, but you can't have a job that requires meticulous detail filled by someone who hates it. You'd be setting them up to fail."

This was all brand-new territory for me. I'd grown up in the construction world believing that if somebody had the skills to swing a hammer or run a site, that's all that mattered. Soft skills like attitude, adaptability, or alignment with a mission felt like an afterthought. But I'd seen the cost of ignoring those qualities.

Timothy kept circling back to one simple message: "Hire slow, fire fast." He hammered it home at least a dozen times. The first half of that phrase was an obvious problem for me. I'd always hired fast because I was afraid of the backlog piling up if I didn't. I was afraid that if I didn't get a crew out there tomorrow, I'd lose the job. But as Timothy pointed out, losing a job is sometimes better than hiring the wrong person and losing your reputation.

"Remember that project manager you held onto for almost a year because you felt bad letting him go?" Timothy asked, reminding me of an older fiasco. That guy had cost me more in rework, schedule incentives, and irritated customers than the salary itself. My excuse for keeping him was always the same: "At least he's here, and I won't have to find a replacement." But that logic backfired.

"So, yeah, if you see it's the wrong person, cut them loose fast," Timothy said. "You're not doing them a favor by keeping them in a role where they can't succeed. And you're not doing your business any favors either."

It was harsh, but I knew he was right. I thought about how many times I'd allowed mediocre or even downright poor performance to slide just because the idea of another job opening made me anxious. Maybe I was afraid of confrontation or worried that no one else would apply. But Timothy believed—and I was starting to believe him—that being honest about someone's fit was actually the kinder route, both for them and the company.

In the spirit of these new insights, I decided to pilot a more structured hiring process for a role we desperately needed: a site foreman for an upcoming commercial build. I wanted to see how well Timothy's suggestions held up in the real world. First, I wrote a clear description of the job, detailing not just the tasks but the qualities that mattered: accountability, teamwork, adaptability under pressure. Then, I posted it in a couple of local industry forums.

I got a handful of responses, but instead of scheduling immediate interviews, I emailed each candidate a quick "pre-qualifying" questionnaire: Why do you want to work here? What's your approach to dealing with unexpected problems on a site? How do you handle conflicts with subs? The answers were revealing. Some folks wrote a sentence or two that felt halfhearted. Others gave thoughtful replies that showed they'd actually read my post.

I narrowed it down to three applicants worth meeting in person. During the interviews, I tested out scenario-based questions Timothy had suggested: "If the supplier drops off the wrong windows a week before the install date, what's your first move?" or "What do you do when a crew member is chronically late?" Their reactions were telling. One candidate got defensive, shifting blame to suppliers or employees—red flag. Another calmly listed the steps he'd take to contain the damage: reorder materials, rework the schedule, update the client, document the error for future lessons. That's what I was hoping to hear: responsibility and problem-solving.

Timothy also convinced me to ask if they'd be open to a short site visit as part of the final step. I got some pushback—one person complained that it was "just more hoops to jump through"—which instantly told me they weren't a good fit. Another candidate, a woman named Denise, said, "Sure, I'd love to see the job site. That'll help me figure out if this is a place where I can excel." I loved that answer, because it showed she was as concerned about fit as I was.

When she showed up on site, I introduced her to a couple of crew members and stepped back to watch. She asked them questions—simple ones about the schedule, material deliveries, and any current snags. Then she hopped into a conversation with one of our carpenters about how they were setting up a tricky door frame. I watched the carpenter's reaction; he didn't roll his eyes or act irritated. He actually seemed to appreciate that she was taking interest. By the end of the walk-through, she'd identified a minor sequencing issue that could have caused a two-day delay, and the crew was already brainstorming a fix.

Timothy's voice played in my head: "Look at how they handle minor chaos." That's exactly what Denise did: she spotted a brewing storm and calmly shifted the crew's approach. I realized I'd never tried anything like this for a new hire in the past. Usually, I'd flip through a résumé, ask a few general questions, and hire them if they seemed polite. This was different. It let me see who she was under real conditions, not just interview chatter.

I offered Denise the job, and she accepted. Over the following weeks, I witnessed firsthand how crucial it was to do these steps properly. She organized daily check-ins, delegated tasks to the right people, and updated me with a quick text if a problem escalated. The difference in atmosphere was staggering. I wasn't out there every hour playing referee. Denise handled it, and I could focus on new contracts and bigger-picture decisions.

Encouraged by this success, I doubled down on Timothy's other ideas. I started using the KOLBE assessment for roles that required quick thinking, like site supers and project managers. I asked a few promising candidates to complete the assessment, and I started noticing patterns in who performed well under pressure. One applicant's résumé looked perfect, but his KOLBE results suggested he struggled with unexpected changes. Sure enough, during a sample site visit, a minor hiccup threw him completely off. Another candidate didn't have the most impressive résumé, but her KOLBE showed she operated in the optimal zone for follow-through and quick start. When I gave her a scenario-based question, she tackled it with a calm confidence that spoke volumes.

I also began using the Strength Assessment from Ministry Insights, particularly for office-based roles where personality alignment was crucial. One candidate's results revealed strong "Implementor" strengths—explaining why scheduling and logistics seemed to come naturally to him. That insight helped me match him with tasks that played to his strengths rather than bogging him down with misaligned responsibilities. Seeing how effective this approach was, I made the assessment a key part of my hiring and team development process.

I'd be lying if I said these assessments were a magic wand. They just helped me see another layer of who a candidate really was. Some old-school guys scoffed at it when I first introduced the idea. They teased me for "overthinking" and said they'd gotten hired back in the day with just a handshake. But for every cynic, there was someone else who said, "Hey, that's interesting—my old boss never cared how I tackled problems, just that I could do them." Those were the people who actually read the instructions and gave thoughtful answers, and they were usually the ones who ended up sticking around.

Of course, a structured process means nothing if I'm not prepared to act on what I learn. Timothy reminded me time and again to trust the data I was collecting. If a candidate had all the right credentials but refused to do a quick on-site test, that was a red flag. If they turned hostile when given a scenario-based question, that was another. I stopped ignoring these clues just because I was eager to fill a role. In the past, desperation would push me to brush aside concerns with a "Well, maybe they'll shape up." But Timothy had hammered home the lesson: if you see big red flags during the hiring phase, it won't magically improve once they're on the payroll.

Along with this new thoroughness came the realization that I needed to respect the candidates who were genuinely good. If I wanted top talent, I had to offer them a fair deal: competitive pay, a safe and organized work environment, and the promise of growth. "Cheap labor will cost you more in the end," Timothy warned me repeatedly. "If you can't afford to pay a decent wage, then you can't afford to hire right now." That was a tough pill to swallow, but it was also a reminder to keep my finances in line with my ambitions.

In the months that followed, the results spoke for themselves. The new hires who made it through these steps were consistently stronger than the ones I'd recruited before. They understood the company's goals, took pride in their craft, and meshed well with the rest of the crew. And if it turned out someone was a poor fit—even after all these screenings—it was easier to let them go because I had tangible reasons: missed deadlines, poor communication, or a failure to handle tasks they'd claimed they could manage.

I also found myself leaning on Timothy's last piece of advice: "Hire slow, fire fast." When a newer hire showed up, I gave them proper training. I tested them in smaller tasks first, then scaled up once they demonstrated they could handle it. If red flags popped up—like repeated late arrivals or an inability to respect safety protocols—I confronted it head-on. If there wasn't improvement, I parted ways. That felt cruel at first, but I realized it was far kinder than letting them hang around in a job they couldn't do.

One day, a young guy named Brandon came on board, fresh out of a trade program. He was eager to learn, but clearly overwhelmed by the pace of a big commercial job. Rather than throwing him in the deep end to see if he'd sink, I paired him with a patient mentor on the crew. Together, they tackled smaller tasks, practicing the rhythms of a job site. Brandon quickly caught on, and his confidence soared. That experience convinced me that "hiring right" also means "training right." You can't just hire someone promising and expect them to read your mind.

At a team meeting one Friday, we were wrapping up a discussion about a new project, with me explaining that we'd be short one site supervisor unless we found someone soon. One of my new leads chimed in, "Don't rush it. Let's do the process." That was when I realized my team had internalized this approach. It wasn't just me preaching about structured hiring; they believed it too because they'd felt the improvement in their day-to-day work.

It's funny how something as basic as a thoughtful hiring process can fundamentally alter a company. Yet looking back, I realized that my old method of "hire whoever's available" had cost me an unsettling amount. All the rework, the lost clients, the wasted hours—none of it had to happen if I'd been more discerning from the start.

By the end of the quarter, I tallied up the improvements. Fewer scheduling conflicts, fewer complaints, and a noticeable bump in revenue because we weren't wasting time or money fixing careless mistakes. Clients were finishing their projects with smiles on their faces, and some even left glowing reviews online. The difference was undeniable. The best part was, we were all happier. We weren't scrounging for replacements every time someone quit in frustration; we were building something that people wanted to be a part of.

Timothy, in his typical understated way, congratulated me. "You've come a long way from that day I found you drowning in résumés," he said, recalling the early meltdown that had triggered this overhaul. I nodded, grateful but also aware that this was just one part of the bigger puzzle—finances, scheduling, and leadership all mattered. But if we didn't get the people part right, everything else was doomed to fail. I knew I had to take hiring more seriously, but I still wasn't entirely sure what roles I needed to fill. That realization would hit me in the weeks ahead.

CHAPTER 8

WHO'S MISSING FROM THE TEAM?

When Timothy scheduled another Zoom call for us on a scorching Friday afternoon, I half expected another conversation about finances. We'd been working on untangling the mess that was my accounting system, and I figured we'd do our usual dance of highlighting missed receipts and debating the benefits of job costing. Instead, he cut right to the chase.

"Tell me what you actually do every day," he said, leaning back in his chair, arms folded. "Walk me through your schedule, hour by hour."

He caught me off guard. But I went for it. "Well, I start by waking up early to check email—mostly because I'm worried someone's going to call out or we'll have a supplier issue. Then I might drive out to a site if I know the crew needs direction. After that, I handle phone calls from clients about changes to their plans or timelines. Somewhere in there, I try to reconcile the books with my part-time bookkeeper, especially if I'm missing an invoice or can't track down a receipt. Then, if there's time, I'll jump to another site in the afternoon." I stopped there, feeling a little breathless.

"Exactly," Timothy said, nodding as if I'd just proved his point. "You've got your hands in everything." He unfolded his arms and leaned forward. "We need to fix that."

I knew he was right, and I'd heard variations of this scolding before. But for some reason, the way he phrased it this time cut deeper. I'd been proud of my involvement in every aspect of the business, convinced that being hands-on showed my commitment. I believed if I wasn't the first and last person on a job site, the whole operation would crumble. Timothy, on the other hand, saw it differently.

"It's not that you can't do all those tasks," he said, "it's that you shouldn't be. You know how to pour concrete, lay tile, frame walls, monitor your bank accounts—you've learned it all the hard way. Great. Now use that knowledge to judge who's good at it, who isn't, and who can learn. You're meant to be overseeing this operation, not tying rebar at six in the morning."

He was getting at something I'd never let sink in: my real job was selling new projects and guiding the company, not physically doing every piece of work. It stung. I'd identified so strongly as a construction guy—someone who could swing a hammer and talk budget in the same breath—that the idea of stepping away from day-to-day tasks felt like turning my back on who I was. But the more Timothy spoke, the more I understood that the business wouldn't survive if I kept treating myself like a catch-all employee.

"Make me a list," he said. "A real list, of all the roles you need to fill if this business is going to run properly. You're not the lone wolf. You need actual job titles that match real responsibilities."

I squirmed in my chair. "All right," I agreed, though I wasn't sure how to start. That evening, I found myself at my dining table, pen in hand, scribbling words onto a notepad. It felt almost embarrassing, like I should've done this years ago. But I pressed on, naming positions that kept popping into my mind.

First, I wrote "Construction Bookkeeper." I'd been fumbling with my accounting since the business began. I'd gone through half a dozen so-called solutions: free software, cheap freelancers, even a cousin who promised to help me organize invoices. None of it stuck, mostly because I was too proud or too paranoid to hand over the books. I realized this had to change. I needed someone who ate numbers for breakfast, who actually got a thrill from balancing accounts. The more I thought about it, the more obvious it seemed: a construction bookkeeper wasn't just optional, it was essential. One missed invoice or incorrectly entered expense could crush my margins, and I'd lived that nightmare more times than I cared to count.

Next, I wrote "Office Manager/Project Coordinator." I paused to wonder if those should be two separate jobs. But for a firm our size, it made sense to roll them together for now. I needed someone who could track materials, schedule subcontractors, handle client calls, and keep the chaos under control. It dawned on me that I'd been trying to do all of that in my spare time. That's why little errors—like forgetting to confirm a materials delivery—kept blowing up into big ones.

I envisioned this person as the command center—an office manager who could coordinate seamlessly with our site superintendent, ensuring someone was there to greet delivery drivers, having the superintendent verify packing slips on-site, and maintaining meticulous records back at the office. They'd be the central hub receiving real-time updates from the field and handling client calls when someone suddenly decided to change the kitchen layout. The office manager wouldn't need to be physically present at every job site—that's what the superintendent was for—but they'd create a communication pipeline that made it feel like they were everywhere at once. It was a tall order, but absolutely vital to bridging the gap between what happened in the field and what got processed at headquarters.

Then I wrote "Site Superintendent." This was where I'd been most reluctant to let go. My identity was wrapped up in the idea of being the lead guy on site. I'd convinced myself that my presence alone kept quality high, that nobody else would catch mistakes as well as I could. But at what cost? I'd be on the phone with a supplier one moment, jumping back to a saw table the next, ignoring half a dozen other fires that needed my attention. By the end of the day, I was exhausted, and the tasks I couldn't finish stacked up like unpaid bills. If I found someone who specialized in running a job site—someone who could coordinate the daily tasks, push the crew to meet goals, and keep an eye on the subtle details of construction—I wouldn't need to micromanage. That freed me up to track down better projects and maintain actual control over the business's direction.

With my list of crucial roles in hand, I called Timothy for guidance on the hiring process. "This is where most contractors fail," he said during our Zoom call. "They get desperate and hire the first person who seems capable. But remember what we discussed—hire the right person for the right seat on the bus. Take your time to find the right people, even if it feels painfully slow."

I started with the construction bookkeeper position, determined to find someone who could bring order to our financial chaos. Timothy had convinced me to use a more structured interview process—one that went beyond the basic resumé review and casual conversation. I crafted detailed questions about accounting practices specific to construction, scenarios involving reconciliation problems, and experience with job costing.

After interviewing five candidates, Maria stood out immediately. Unlike the others who spoke in generalities, she brought examples of how she'd organized accounting for a similar-sized contractor, complete with unnamed reports showing before-and-after comparisons of their books.

"Tell me about a time you found an error that saved a company money," I asked during our second interview.

Maria didn't hesitate. "At my previous job, I noticed a pattern of double-billing from a supplier. They were sending invoices under slightly different job numbers for the same deliveries. I used a reconciliation process that caught about $15,000 in duplicate charges over six months."

Her methodical approach to problem-solving matched exactly what Timothy had described as essential for this role. When I offered her the position, she asked thoughtful questions about our current systems and challenges, already thinking about how she would tackle the mess I'd created.

For the office manager/project coordinator role, James came through a recommendation from a subcontractor I trusted. On paper, he looked solid—experience with scheduling, vendor management, and client communication. But Timothy had taught me that interview performance didn't always translate to on-the-job success.

"Have him walk through a typical project day," Timothy suggested. "See how he handles multiple demands at once."

I took his advice, creating a simulation exercise where James had to juggle incoming calls about material delays, schedule changes, and a challenging client situation—all while organizing delivery logistics for an upcoming project.

James approached the exercise with a calm efficiency that impressed me. He prioritized issues quickly, documented everything in a simple spreadsheet he created on the spot, and maintained a professional demeanor even when I deliberately threw in challenging curveballs.

"I noticed you didn't get flustered when I mentioned the delayed concrete delivery," I said afterward.

He smiled. "In my experience, panicking never pours concrete any faster. Better to immediately work on solutions—calling alternate suppliers, adjusting the day's schedule to work on different tasks, and being transparent with everyone affected."

That practical mindset sold me. James had the perfect blend of organization and adaptability that we needed.

The site superintendent role proved the most challenging. I'd interviewed several candidates with impressive technical skills, but finding someone who could lead a crew while maintaining our quality standards seemed impossible. Timothy suggested I move beyond traditional interviews for this position.

"Have your final candidates spend half a day on site," he advised. "Watch how they interact with the crew, how they assess work quality, how they solve problems in real time."

This approach led me to Mark. He'd spent fifteen years in the field and had supervised crews for about half that time. During his site visit, I watched as he naturally fell into a mentoring role with a younger carpenter who was struggling with a complex framing detail. Without being asked, Mark picked up a pencil, sketched out the solution on a piece of scrap wood, and helped the carpenter understand not just what to do, but why it mattered.

Later, when I intentionally pointed out a window installation that was slightly off, Mark didn't just agree with me—he pulled out a level, confirmed the issue, and immediately outlined three possible fixes, weighing the pros and cons of each approach.

"What impressed me most," I told Timothy later, "was that he didn't throw anyone under the bus. He focused on the solution, not the blame."

"That's leadership," Timothy replied. "Technical skills can be taught, but that kind of character is what you need in a superintendent."

Within a month of bringing Maria, James, and Mark on board, I could already see positive changes. Maria had begun organizing our financial records, establishing clear processes for expense tracking, and setting up real-time budget reports that finally gave me visibility into our true financial position. James had streamlined our scheduling, creating a centralized system that prevented the double-bookings and resource conflicts that had plagued us for years. And Mark had established consistent quality standards across our job sites, reducing rework and improving crew morale.

We had taken our time, been thorough, and the results were already showing. But we still had gaps to fill, and I wanted to understand exactly what was missing from my team. By the time I finished my list, it was obvious what needed to happen next—I had to ensure these new team members could work effectively together.

"Good," he said. "Now we need to focus on filling these roles properly, not just any warm body. Think about what each position really needs."

I took a breath.

"Let's discuss what each of these key team members should be doing on a daily basis," Timothy suggested. "We need to make sure they're working effectively together and that you're not still trying to do their jobs."

We started with Maria, our construction bookkeeper. While she was excellent with numbers and had already brought order to our financial chaos, Timothy pointed out that I needed to give her more responsibility. "Are you still approving every expense?" he asked. "Or are you letting her flag anomalies and bring them to your attention?"

I admitted I was still micromanaging the financials more than necessary. "She's more than capable," I said, "but old habits die hard."

Timothy shook his head. "You've got someone who takes pride in her work. Let her do it. Set clear boundaries about what requires your approval—maybe expenses over a certain threshold—but otherwise, step back."

We moved on to James, our office manager. I explained how he had revolutionized our scheduling, but I was still jumping in whenever a client called with changes. "It's like I don't trust that he'll handle it right," I confessed.

"That's exactly the problem," Timothy said. "You hired him because he has the skills to coordinate and problem-solve. But if you keep swooping in, you're undermining his authority and wasting the talent you're paying for."

Finally, we discussed Mark, our site superintendent. I'd been visiting job sites daily, sometimes multiple times, often giving instructions that contradicted what Mark had told the crew. "I just can't help myself," I admitted. "I see something I would do differently, and I jump in."

Timothy frowned. "That's the fastest way to lose a good superintendent. He can't lead if you're constantly second-guessing him. Either trust him to run the site, or admit you don't believe he's right for the job."

The truth hit hard: I had assembled a solid team but wasn't letting them do what I'd hired them for. I was still trying to be the bookkeeper, the office manager, and the site superintendent all at once.

"So what's really missing from your team?" Timothy asked pointedly.

I thought for a moment. "Trust," I said finally. "I'm not truly letting them do their jobs."

"Exactly," Timothy nodded. "And what else?"

After some reflection, I realized what he was getting at. "Clear boundaries. I need to define where my role ends and theirs begins."

"That's right," Timothy said. "And there's one more thing. What should you be focusing on if they're handling all these other responsibilities?"

The answer was clear: "Business development. Finding new clients, nurturing relationships, and planning our growth."

Timothy smiled. "That's the role that's been missing—yours. You've been so busy doing everyone else's job that you haven't been doing your own efficiently."

This conversation marked a turning point. I began scheduling weekly team meetings to improve communication among Maria, James, and Mark. Instead of micromanaging, I asked for updates and offered guidance only when needed. I created a simple document outlining responsibilities and shared it with everyone, so there'd be no question about who handled what.

The results were immediate. Maria took full ownership of our financials, creating reports that gave me clear insights without requiring me to dig through every transaction. James developed a streamlined system for scheduling and client communications, freeing me from daily logistics. Mark established a rhythm on the job sites that kept crews productive and on schedule without my constant presence.

With these key players handling their areas of expertise, I finally had the bandwidth to focus on what I should have been doing all along: drumming up new business and steering our company's growth.

The shift became apparent when an old client—someone who'd sworn never to work with me again after a botched remodel—reached out about a new addition on his property. In our meeting, I confidently explained how our team would handle his project: Maria monitoring costs, James co-ordinating logistics, and Mark ensuring quality on-site. The client peppered me with questions, trying to find weaknesses in our approach. But now I had real answers, backed by a team I trusted. He signed the contract on the spot.

That project unfolded smoothly. I visited occasionally but resisted the urge to micromanage. Instead, I focused on cultivating relationships for future work. When Timothy checked in toward the end of the project, I shared how different things felt.

"I walked the site this morning," I told him. "Mark was handling a minor adjustment with a subcontractor. James had already confirmed tomorrow's deliveries. Maria had the latest budget report ready for my review. And I was free to meet with a potential new client afterward."

Timothy grinned. "Feels different, doesn't it?"

"It really does," I replied, and I meant it wholeheartedly. The team was no longer missing vital roles—including my own as the leader rather than the doer of all things.

CHAPTER 9

WHEN TO BRING PEOPLE ON

I was standing by the back door of our field office, brushing sawdust off my pants. The day had been grueling. I felt drained, yet I could sense something shifting in the company. My phone vibrated, reminding me of my virtual meeting with Timothy. I walked into my office, sat down at my computer, and clicked the link. Then, Timothy appeared.

"All right, what's on your mind?" he asked.

I shrugged. "I'm thinking about whether it's time to scale up again."

Timothy nodded. "Figured as much. Let's talk it through. You've done a great job straightening out a lot of the chaos—getting the right people, putting systems in place. So the question is, how do you know when to bring on more?"

I leaned back in my chair. "A few months ago, I wouldn't have believed we could handle the workload we do now. Everything runs smoother. The new hires we've made are pulling their weight, and I'm not buried in twenty different tasks before lunch. I guess part of me is saying, 'If a little expansion helped, why not bring in more people and jump to the next level?'"

"Hiring more isn't automatically good," he said, measured. "It's about timing, about having the cash flow and the operational readiness to support those extra salaries from day one."

I remembered the first time he'd brought up the idea of employees as "income-producing assets." At the time, it felt like a stiff way to talk about human beings, but I got the point: each hire should add immediate value, not just fill a gap out of desperation. And if you don't handle that carefully—if you hire too many too soon—you burn cash, morale, and potentially your reputation.

Sighing, I slumped forward. "That's the tricky part. I'm juggling these urges to seize every opportunity with a fear of overreaching. I can't forget what happened last year when I brought in a whole crew of temps for that big renovation. On paper, it made sense—more hands, faster work, right?"

Timothy responded with a slight shake of his head. "How'd that turn out?"

"Awful," I admitted. "They were enthusiastic but unskilled, and I was too swamped to train them properly. Next thing I knew, we had miscut lumber, improperly tied steel, hung doors incorrectly, and half the job had to be redone. Plus, I had to dip into a line of credit to cover payroll when the timeline went long. That set me back for months."

Timothy clicked his tongue. “Exactly. You had the project, but not the right people. And unskilled labor might look cheaper, but the cost of training and mistakes can eat you alive. Expansion only works if each new hire is productive from the jump, or at least very close to it. If they aren’t, you risk blowing your budget on training, rework, or carrying them while they get up to speed.”

I thought about how, in construction, the margin for error can be razor-thin. A single mistake in framing or a supplier who can’t deliver on time can wreck a schedule. The thought of repeating that fiasco—of piling on more help than the business could handle—made me uneasy.

“You know, I’m not telling you to be stingy. Skilled folks will cost you more up front, but you avoid that drawn-out learning curve. If your finances aren’t locked in enough to handle that cost, you either push for more operating capital or wait.”

He’d given me the same advice before in smaller doses, but somehow, it resonated more now that I saw the difference good hires made. Maria, our construction bookkeeper, had brought clarity to our financial records within weeks. James, our office manager, reduced the chaos of scheduling and field calls. Mark, our superintendent, took an enormous load off my shoulders on-site. Each of them had delivered immediate results, just as Timothy said they would.

But there was also the very real concern of cash flow. Even with everything running more smoothly, we weren’t sitting on piles of money. If I didn’t time new hires properly, I’d either have to float them on credit or scramble to find extra work to keep them busy. That was exactly the scenario I wanted to avoid—robbing Peter to pay Paul or taking on uncertain jobs just to cover payroll.

Through the computer screen, I saw Timothy point toward a photo in his office that showed a half-finished set of framing. "Think of that structure as your business plan. Every board is a role or resource you've put in place. If you try to bolt on a second floor before the first is stable, you risk the entire thing collapsing."

I had to laugh at the construction analogy. "So you're saying I shouldn't add the second floor until the first is fully braced and I know I have enough materials to finish the job?"

He nodded. "Exactly. This is where forecasting comes in. You need to know how much work is lined up, what the cash flow looks like, and which roles are truly necessary. Don't hire just because you see a temporary spike in demand. Hire because your data shows you can sustain that new role over the long haul."

At that point, I recalled how I'd used to rely on gut instincts about future projects. If a client said they might have a job for me in six months, I'd jump the gun, hire more guys, and bank on that job materializing. That rarely ended well. Now, thanks to Timothy's insistence on tracking everything and Maria's organizational skills with our books, I had actual data that estimated our monthly income based on confirmed contracts, not just hopeful leads. That alone changed how I viewed expansion.

"That means we hold off on certain hires until we're sure the workload justifies them, right?" I asked.

"Absolutely," Timothy replied. "You also have to consider how long it'll take to get them fully productive. If the new person is skilled, they'll hit the ground running sooner. If not, factor in the training period and the potential for errors. That's where a lot of contractors slip up—they underestimate how much it costs to bring someone up to speed."

I'd learned that the hard way. Training novices can be beneficial if you have a solid mentor in place and a schedule that can handle a little give. But if the job is critical, or the timeline is tight, that "cheap labor" ends up costing more.

We sat for another minute. I listened to the sounds of the site winding down for the day. Workers were cleaning up, stacking materials, and loading them back into trucks.

Timothy cleared his throat. "There's another angle here: mismanaging change orders or timelines. If you expand too fast and a project hits a snag—like a major design tweak or a client who can't make payments on time—you'll be stuck with an oversized team waiting around. Meanwhile, your overhead keeps burning your cash."

"So how do I read this in the context of adding more staff?" I asked, gesturing at the numbers.

Timothy ran his finger down the columns. "Look at the consistent projects, the ones that are locked in with signed contracts and deposits. Assess how much labor each job needs and how soon you'll see cash from them. If you have a cushion that allows you to bring on a skilled worker without scrambling for a loan, you're probably in good shape. But if you notice that your revenue for the next few months is uncertain, or heavily dependent on a single big job that hasn't fully closed, that's riskier."

He then circled a figure representing our current overhead. "Think about how another salary—plus insurance, plus benefits (which we call labor burden)—will affect that number. If the new hire isn't generating productivity that covers their cost quickly, you'll find yourself slipping into the red. And as you've learned, bridging shortfalls with credit can become a cycle."

I nodded, remembering all the times I'd used short-term loans or credit cards just to float payroll, praying a check would arrive in time to cover it. That vicious cycle left me gasping for air more than once.

Timothy settled back in his chair. "Hiring is supposed to make you money in the long run, not sink you. So weigh each hire carefully—what will they do, how soon can they do it, how much will it cost to get them going, and how much can you realistically expect to earn because of their contribution?"

"But what if I'm chasing bigger projects that require more staff?" I asked. "Couldn't I line up the hires in anticipation of those jobs?"

He pressed his lips together. "Sure, if you have the financial reserves and the project is near-certain. But if you're gambling on a job that's not locked in, you risk paying salaries for people with nothing to do. Or you end up forcing them into smaller jobs that don't really need that many bodies, driving up overhead and cutting profit margins."

I thought about how I used to equate "more staff" with "more capacity," as if I could magically handle a flood of new work. But building capacity isn't just about adding heads; it's about adding the right heads at the right time. If you pile on staff prematurely, you either run them idle or scramble to feed them projects that might not fit your core focus, leading to compromise on quality or margins.

Timothy pointed to the overhead figure again. "Remember, every extra hire adds to your base expenses. If your overhead is too high, you'll need a steady stream of projects just to break even. That's a stressful place to be—one hiccup, and you're behind the eight ball. It's better to grow slower and maintain a comfortable overhead than to balloon and collapse under the weight of payroll obligations."

I typed a note to myself: "Check overhead ratio monthly. Update Timothy on potential hires only after verifying cash flow buffer."

He smirked. "Your note-taking has improved. Guess you're really committed to avoiding old mistakes now."

I chuckled softly. "I have to be. The days of seat-of-my-pants hiring taught me enough lessons."

Most of the crew had headed home. As we started wrapping up our call, I asked Timothy one more thing that had been nagging at me. "So, let's say everything lines up and I do hire someone. How do I know if I made the right call?"

"Watch the metrics from day one," he said. "Did they improve efficiency? Did they help complete tasks that free you up to do other valuable work? Did the job flow get smoother, or are you just paying extra salary with no noticeable uptick in performance? You'll see it in the bottom line, but also in day-to-day operations."

I nodded. It reminded me of how Mark, our site superintendent, had proven his worth almost immediately by cutting down rework and boosting morale. "So if I don't see improvement in the short term, that means it's probably a sign I moved too soon or picked the wrong person."

Timothy paused. "Exactly. Sometimes you hire a great person at the wrong time; sometimes you hire at the right time but the person's not up to par. Either way, pay attention and correct it fast. Don't let it fester."

After Timothy left the call, I sat there a moment longer, replaying the conversation in my mind. Everything he said lined up with mistakes I'd made in the past. I'd been guilty of hiring unskilled labor to handle a workload I wasn't even sure I had the resources to cover, and I'd let overhead balloon until I was drowning in debt. The difference now was that I had real financial data at my fingertips and a plan to evaluate each new hire's immediate impact.

We had the systems, the crew, and a more disciplined approach. If I stuck to Timothy's advice—treating each hire as an investment and verifying that the business could afford them—I could scale without losing everything I'd worked so hard to rebuild.

That night, I sat at the kitchen table. I flipped through the next month's project schedule, marking which days were already fully booked and which days had some slack. Normally, seeing that slack would make me itch to hire more people and fill the schedule with more projects. But now I asked myself whether the upcoming jobs truly demanded additional staff, or if the team I had could handle them efficiently.

I realized that if I did want to expand, I needed a clear rationale. Maybe we'd secured a large commercial project that our current crew couldn't manage alone. Or maybe we'd branched into a specialty service—like custom millwork—that required a new kind of expert. In those cases, bringing someone in made sense, as long as the numbers and timelines checked out. But hiring just because I "had a feeling" business was picking up? That was a trap I'd fallen into before.

I also considered the age-old debate: hiring someone who's semi-skilled and training them up versus paying more for someone who's already top-notch. In a calmer moment, I saw it as a matter of risk tolerance. If the schedule was tight and mistakes would be catastrophic, I should find a well-established professional. If I had a stable pipeline and a reliable mentorship system, I might bring on a less experienced worker who showed promise. But either way, I wouldn't compromise on the fundamental requirement: that each hire eventually pays for themselves by creating value and helping the company thrive.

A few weeks later, I put all of Timothy's advice to the test when I got a lead on a high-end commercial renovation that looked promising. Before jumping, I scheduled another call with Timothy to project our cash flow for the next three months. He guided me through the process, showing me how to account for the cost of hiring two skilled tradespeople to accommodate the additional workload.

"Let's look at your confirmed projects and their payment schedules," Timothy said, walking me through the analysis. "Then we'll overlay the projected costs for these new hires—not just salary, but benefits, taxes, equipment, and any training time."

We ran the numbers meticulously, factoring in every variable. Timothy helped me see that if we landed the job, we'd have the revenue to support those hires comfortably—provided we structured the payments properly and the client's credit checks didn't raise any alarms.

"The key is to be realistic," Timothy emphasized. "Factor in worst-case scenarios: payments coming in late, unexpected expenses, delays. If you can still support these hires even when things don't go perfectly, that's when you know you're ready."

I asked Mark to evaluate the site and draft a rough timeline. He came back with a clear breakdown: with two more skilled carpenters, we could finish a month earlier than usual, possibly opening us up to another job right after. That sealed the deal. I didn't just "feel" it was the right time; the data confirmed it. We made an offer to two experienced tradespeople who'd come highly recommended from a subcontractor we'd used in the past. By day two on the new job, they were already saving us a ton of time, tackling complex framing details that might've slowed down a less experienced pair.

Each evening that week, I noted how the new hires were affecting our progress. They integrated well with the existing crew, and I could see that our timeline was indeed shaping up faster than anticipated. The bonus was that I didn't have to go home panicking about how to cover their wages. Our plan ensured we had the buffer for it.

Timothy, of course, checked in. "So, any regrets on bringing them aboard?" he asked.

"None," I replied. "I actually wish I'd had this approach sooner. It would've saved me a ton of stress if I'd waited for the right moment to expand in the past, instead of blindly scaling whenever I felt overwhelmed."

He gave a small grin. "That's what I like to hear. Keep a tight watch on costs, though. Even great hires become a burden if your next job doesn't pan out or if you go too long without new business."

Chapter 10

The Importance of Training

I'd spent years convinced that if I hired the right people—carpenters who could handle power tools, an office manager who knew scheduling, a bookkeeper who could spot accounting errors—the rest would take care of itself. It seemed logical: find good folks, give them a quick rundown, and let them loose. But after a string of mishaps on the job and mounting frustrations from the crew, Timothy made me realize just how flawed that assumption really was. Hiring was just the first step. Training them to excel was where the real challenge began.

I still remember the day everything clicked. We were reviewing a recent project: a simple bathroom remodel that had somehow ballooned into a giant headache. Materials went missing, the subcontractors complained about unclear instructions, and the new apprentice kept mixing the grout inconsistently because nobody showed him the technique. By the time we finally wrapped, everyone was exhausted, and the client was unimpressed. Timothy listened to me list off the issues and leaned back in his chair.

"You're expecting them to know what 'quality' means," he said. "But have you shown them?"

He had a point. My idea of "quality" was ingrained in me after years of mistakes and late-night lessons. I'd never taken the time to translate that experience into a structured process that new people could learn without stumbling around. Sure, I could handle a job like that on autopilot, but someone fresh to the team had no roadmap.

"If you want them to meet high standards," Timothy added, "you have to spell out what those standards are. Otherwise, you'll keep running into these same problems."

That observation hit me harder than I expected. I'd always prided myself on "leading by example," but it was impossible to be everywhere at once. And as the company grew, I found myself juggling more responsibilities—meeting with clients, monitoring finances, scouting new projects—while my crew tried to piece together my vision on-site. The result was confusion, rework, and unnecessary stress.

"Training is your insurance," Timothy explained. "It prevents the same mistakes from happening over and over. You invest the time up front, and you'll save yourself a world of hurt later."

He introduced me to a concept he called "training for excellence," which meant more than just giving a quick orientation. It was about continuous, hands-on learning that set clear expectations at every step. Timothy had seen too many contractors treat training like an afterthought—sending new hires into the field with a pat on the back and hoping they'd pick it up. He wanted me to break that cycle.

"There are tools you could eventually use to record short videos of how you do things," he said. "Simple instructions, step by step—how you measure a cut, how you fill out a timesheet, how you label materials."

He also mentioned a platform that could help organize all those videos, quizzes, and checklists into a structured program. "When you're ready to commit to proper training, we'll explore the right technology to support it." "Don't worry if you're not a tech wizard," Timothy reassured me. "There are consultants for that. You just need to be willing to explain exactly how your business does things. Then capture it, so no one has to guess."

The idea of filming myself measuring cuts or explaining a blueprint felt almost comical. But when I looked back on the dozens of times I'd had to re-explain tasks to new hires, or the arguments that stemmed from unclear procedures, it no longer seemed so ridiculous. I realized that every repeated explanation, every botched job, was time (and money) lost. Documenting tasks once in a clear, digestible format might free me from having that conversation a hundred times.

I decided to start small. One of our biggest pain points was a sloppy approach to timesheets. Payroll errors were constant, and people argued about recorded hours. So, I pulled out my phone and recorded a short screen capture where I walked through filling out an online timesheet. I explained what each field meant, how to add project codes, and the importance of accuracy for both payroll and job costing. It was a three-minute clip, but it beat repeating myself every week.

I sent it to a couple of new hires, telling them to watch and then follow it next time they clocked their hours. One of them told me later, "That really helped. I didn't realize how crucial it was to match the hours to the right project." It was a minor success, but enough to convince me that Timothy was onto something.

He also stressed that training wasn't just about technical skills. "You need to teach attitude," he said. "Construction is stressful. If you don't show them your approach to handling setbacks—like delayed materials or a client who keeps changing their mind—they'll default to panic or blame."

"Doesn't that feel too corporate?" I asked, suddenly picturing some sterile HR meeting.

"Only if you make it that way," Timothy replied. "Keep it practical and real. Instead of giving them a lecture, show them the real examples from your jobs. Walk them through a scenario where materials show up late and how you'd resolve it—who do you call, how do you reschedule tasks, how do you communicate to the client?"

I liked that approach: no fluff, just a clear demonstration of how we operate. I started mapping out a training plan in my notebook, listing topics that seemed most urgent. We needed safety guidelines for new hires before they ever stepped onto a site, instructions for running and maintaining equipment, an overview of basic scheduling principles, and a sense of our cultural values—showing up on time, respecting clients, cleaning up at the end of the day.

The more I thought about it, the more I realized a single person had to oversee all this. Whether it was me or someone else, training had to be someone's specific job. If we treated it like a side task, it would keep getting shuffled around. Timothy suggested I find an "office manager or training facilitator"—someone who could wrangle the content, schedule training sessions, and update materials as we grew.

"Think of it as an investment," he said. "If you're not training your people properly, you'll pay for it through rework, turnover, or accidents."

So I tapped James, our office manager, to take on that role, at least temporarily. He was organized, cool under pressure, and had a knack for explaining things clearly. We set up a couple of hours each week where James would collaborate with me on building out a library of training materials—everything from short videos to step-by-step guides. It wasn't glamorous, but I quickly saw how vital it was.

When a new hire arrived, we could actually say, "Watch these five videos first. Then we'll walk you through them in person, answer questions, and do a quick test to make sure you've got it." It felt professional, almost like we were leveling up from a mom-and-pop operation to something more established. And guess what? New hires responded positively. They appreciated having a structured intro instead of being thrown onto a site with zero context.

Of course, it wasn't all smooth sailing. I recorded a training video on reading blueprints that was so boring I nearly fell asleep editing it. I realized I sounded like a droning teacher, reading from a script. So, I redid it, this time more conversational, actually showing an example blueprint on the screen and pointing out common pitfalls. Timothy watched the new version and gave me a thumbs-up, saying, "Now you sound like someone who's teaching an actual person, not just reading text."

I also found that in-person follow-ups were crucial. A video or a quiz was great for initial understanding, but real learning happened when someone asked, "What if the dimensions in the blueprint don't match the actual site conditions?" and we'd walk through potential solutions. That's how you take theoretical knowledge and make it practical.

As we kept going, Timothy reminded me not to aim for perfection. "You can always revise," he said. "The important thing is to have something in place. If you wait until you have the perfect training curriculum, you'll never start."

So, we started small, focusing on the most immediate pain points—safety, timesheets, basic tool operations, job site etiquette. Then we added more specialized modules, like advanced framing techniques or how to handle unexpected design changes without throwing the project off schedule. Over time, we built a modest but growing library of resources.

The changes in the field were noticeable. Fewer frantic phone calls, fewer repeated mistakes, and fewer last-minute scrambles because someone didn't know the protocol. Mark, our site superintendent, told me it felt like the new hires had a "foundation" to stand on, so he could focus on the day's tasks rather than babysitting them. Even our seasoned workers started referencing the training materials if they forgot something or wanted to brush up—like the steps to operate a piece of rented equipment they hadn't used in months.

The biggest payoff, though, came from reduced turnover. Before, we had a cycle of new people leaving within weeks, overwhelmed by the chaos. Now they had clarity from day one. They understood what we expected, they had the tools to do their jobs, and they felt supported. That sense of competence and confidence kept them around longer, which meant less time spent on recruitment, interviews, and onboarding.

One afternoon, a new carpenter named Annie told me she'd never had an employer explain so clearly how the project flow worked. "My last boss just threw me into the job," she said. "If I messed up, he'd yell, but he never told me what he actually wanted. Here, you gave me a video on how you expect interior walls to be framed, and I watched it at home before my first day. It made a world of difference."

Hearing that was a lightbulb moment for me. Training wasn't just about protecting my bottom line—it was about respecting the people who came on board. It showed them I cared enough to give them direction, not just grunt work. That respect fed into a stronger culture overall.

Of course, the process is never finished. We kept noticing gaps in our training as new situations arose. The first time we did a major historical renovation, we discovered our basic training didn't cover the extra precautions for preserving original woodwork. So, we filmed a quick segment on how to treat antique trim, emphasizing the different approach from standard drywall or modern lumber. Next time we tackled a historical project, we were ready.

Timothy also encouraged us to "train the trainer." In other words, I wasn't the only one creating materials. If James excelled at scheduling, he should record a tutorial on how to handle a schedule board. If Mark was a pro at daily job site briefings, let him demonstrate in a video. We wanted each expert sharing their best knowledge with the rest of the team. That way, our training library grew from multiple perspectives, not just mine.

I also realized the importance of following up after a new hire completed the initial training. I'd have a short meeting with them to see if they had any questions or if something in the training didn't align with on-site reality. Those talks helped us catch inconsistencies. Sometimes we had to update a video or clarify a quiz question. Other times, the new hire just needed a quick demonstration in person. But that loop of "train, apply, get feedback, refine" made our system stronger every time.

One of the best decisions I made was setting up a monthly "brown-bag" session—essentially a casual lunch where we'd review one topic in depth. Sometimes it was a safety refresher, sometimes a new construction technique, sometimes an administrative update like how to use a new project management app. These lunches kept the culture of learning alive, showing everyone that training wasn't a one-and-done event. If we found a better way to do something, we'd update our materials and let the team know at the next session.

During our monthly team training, I recorded the session where we discussed our new job costing approach. When I shared the video with Timothy during our next Zoom call, his face lit up with genuine approval. "These training sessions are gold," he said, leaning closer to his webcam. "I can see exactly what I hoped you'd create—a team that's openly sharing knowledge instead of guarding it like some trade secret. The way your foreman jumped in to explain that calculation to the newer guys? That's how you scale a construction business without losing quality. Send me more of these videos. I love seeing the culture you're building."

It reminded me of how I used to handle a problem: if something went wrong, I'd fix it myself or bark orders for someone else to handle it. Now, we tried to anticipate those issues in our training materials or at these lunch sessions, so everyone knew what to do before trouble hit.

Sure, it cost money upfront. I hired a Trainual consultant for a couple of months to help organize and brand our training modules. I bought a decent camera and microphone to improve the video quality. We spent man-hours filming and editing. If you'd asked me two years ago whether I wanted to "waste" so much time documenting tasks I already knew by heart, I would have laughed. But after seeing the results—in reduced rework, fewer misunderstandings, and employees who felt empowered—I'd do it again in a heartbeat.

Another unexpected benefit was how training reinforced our culture. The videos and quizzes we created didn't just teach tasks; they taught our philosophy. Every module, whether it was about installing a window correctly or handling a client complaint, carried the underlying message: "We do things right, we communicate, we own our work." Gradually, that ethos became part of everyone's mindset, new hires and veterans alike.

As new hires came in, I noticed they ramped up to full productivity faster than before. We didn't have that awkward period of six or eight weeks where they were lost, trying to pick up on unwritten rules. Now, they had a reference: a set of materials that spelled out the rules in plain language.

Timothy summarized it well in one of our catch-up meetings. He said, "You're not just handing them instructions; you're handing them *confidence*." That stuck with me. Confidence is huge in this line of work. A crew member who's unsure will hesitate, double-guess, or hide mistakes. A confident crew member takes initiative, speaks up when they see an issue, and trusts their training.

One day, I was walking the site and saw two apprentices—neither had been with us more than a month—calmly handling a small layout error on a blueprint. Instead of yelling for a supervisor, they cross-referenced a quick video we'd made on reading blueprints and used the outlined approach to shift a wall a few inches. I asked Mark later if he had to fix anything, and he shook his head. "They nailed it perfectly," he said. "I just double-checked their measurements, and it was good to go."

That moment might seem small, but it felt huge. It showed me how far we'd come from the days when a missing inch on a plan could trigger hours of confusion. Training gave those apprentices the means to solve a problem themselves, saving the entire crew time and frustration.

Of course, we continue to adapt. A training program isn't static. We keep an eye on new technology, building codes, or methods that could improve the way we work. Whenever we add something new—like a different insulation technique or a software tool to manage site logs—we create a short module. The library grows, but it remains orderly thanks to James's oversight.

On a personal level, training also freed me from micromanagement. Once upon a time, I felt I had to hover over everyone to ensure quality. Now, I can trust they've seen how we want things done and tested their understanding. If they hit a snag, they can revisit the training or ask a targeted question. I'm not stuck re-explaining fundamentals.

Timothy occasionally jokes that I've become a "training evangelist," but I can't help it—I've seen the difference it makes in the daily grind. We're more efficient, our turnover is lower, and clients notice the professionalism. They don't see a bunch of frantic workers guessing. They see a coordinated team that knows what's happening and why.

The final piece of Timothy's advice was this: "Never assume training is finished. As long as you're in business, you'll be updating something." That keeps me on my toes. Whether it's refining our safety protocols or teaching a brand-new material handling method, I see training as an ongoing investment. We don't wait for an emergency or a cascade of mistakes to fix something; we try to be proactive and share knowledge before it becomes critical.

Now, I can't imagine running this operation without it. Every time a new crew member fits seamlessly into the team, or a complex job site hums along without a million minor mistakes, I think, "This is why we do it." It's not about fancy buzzwords or corporate slogans. It's about giving people the knowledge and tools to meet high expectations. And in construction, where one miscalculation can cost thousands or even tens of thousands, that knowledge can be the difference between profit and disaster.

So, when someone asks me how we turned things around—how we went from a chaotic, fire-fighting outfit to a smoother-running operation—I tell them the truth: first, we hired people who matched our values and skill needs, but then we trained them properly. We invested in them with clear, consistent processes. We used technology to capture our best practices, turning them into something anyone could learn from. And we assigned a dedicated person to shepherd this continuous process. Those steps transformed the day-to-day reality of the company more than any single piece of equipment or any fancy new marketing strategy ever could.

These days, I walk onto a job site and see workers referencing tablets or phones to rewatch a quick training snippet on a tricky installation. I see them answer each other's questions by saying, "Check the training module on that—there's a video that shows you exactly how," rather than shrugging or guessing. The conversations have changed. There's a shared understanding that training isn't just for newbies; it's for all of us, whenever we confront a new challenge.

Timothy occasionally reminds me, "This isn't static. You'll keep adding, editing, refining." And he's right. But I welcome that challenge now. We've built a foundation where continuous training feels normal, not like an intrusion. It's how we keep pace with changing materials, codes, and expectations.

If I could give the past-me a piece of advice, it would be this: "Stop expecting people to read your mind. Show them, step by step, how you want things done, and keep reinforcing it until it's second nature." It's easy to assume that what's obvious to you is obvious to them, but it rarely is. The time spent clarifying up front is dwarfed by the time you'll save in rework or disputes.

And that's how I've come to see training: it's not an optional line item on some budget, but a core investment in the future. It's insurance against costly errors, a tool for employee retention, and a path to sustainable growth. Timothy knew that from the start, and it took me a while to catch on, but once I did, everything changed.

Timothy calls it "training for excellence." I call it a game-changer. It took me a long time to see it, but now I can't imagine running this business any other way.

Chapter 11

What Tools Does a Modern Construction Business Need?

Now that we had solidified our team structure and financial processes, it was time to address the technology gap Timothy had been preparing me for. All those manual spreadsheets, basic tracking systems, and makeshift solutions I'd been using were about to be upgraded to a proper technology stack. Even in construction, staying modern is a necessity. It was a rainy morning, the kind that makes everything look muted and paused, when I sat down for one of our weekly Zoom calls with Timothy. The screen loaded for a moment, and there he was, this time in front of a backdrop that included a whiteboard scribbled with notes and diagrams. He looked directly into the camera.

"By now, I'm sure you've figured out that modern construction isn't really about hammers and nails alone anymore," Timothy began. "It's really all about using the right tools to streamline your work, keep everyone on the same page, and ultimately, make your job easier." I leaned forward, curious and admittedly a bit skeptical. I'd been running my business the old-fashioned way for years—relying on experience, gut instinct, and a healthy dose of stubbornness. But as Timothy started listing off the many, necessary names like BuilderTrend, QuickBooks Online, Dext, Gusto Payroll, and Bill.com, I sensed that I was in for another important lesson.

"BuilderTrend, as you know, is one of my favorites," he explained. "It's such a great project management tool that's designed specifically for construction. It helps you track schedules, manage change orders, even communicate with clients and subcontractors—all in one place."

He leaned forward, tapping his screen excitedly. "But here's what changed everything for us—their time clock solution. Our crews now clock in and out right from their phones on the job site, and the system automatically allocates their hours and labor burden rates to each specific job. No more paper timesheets disappearing into truck consoles or showing up crumpled and coffee-stained a week later."

I nodded, remembering those chaotic payroll days. Timothy continued, "Then on Thursday afternoons, with just a few clicks, we export those accurate timesheets from BuilderTrend straight into Gusto for payroll. What used to take an entire day of chasing people down now happens in minutes."

I thought back to those frantic days when I'd scramble through emails, phone calls, and handwritten notes trying to keep a project on track. BuilderTrend had become our digital command center, a hub where every detail—from schedules to change orders to precise labor costs—was right at our fingertips.

I admitted, with a smile, that the idea of managing everything from my phone or computer felt almost futuristic. "So you're saying I can see the whole project, from budgeting to scheduling, without running back and forth between job sites?" I asked. Timothy nodded. "Exactly. When everyone knows what's happening, delays and miscommunications vanish almost as quickly as they appear."

Then came QuickBooks Online, which Timothy introduced as the backbone of modern accounting. "QuickBooks Online isn't just for accountants," he said during our call. "It's actually a tool for business owners to get a real-time picture of their finances. You can easily track income and expenses. And because QuickBooks is online, you can access it from anywhere—whether you're on a job site or at home." I couldn't help but think back to those (surprisingly memorable) frantic nights spent reconciling endless spreadsheets and stacks of receipts. Seems I'll never forget them, though I'm glad they're in the rearview. In any case, QuickBooks Online promised a level of simplicity I'd only ever dreamed of.

This is about tracking and managing receipts to properly job cost. And that's where Dext came in. Timothy explained, "Dext is an expense tracking tool that lets you capture receipts on the fly. Instead of rummaging through shoeboxes of crumpled paper receipts, you just snap a photo with your phone, and Dext does the rest. It automatically categorizes and uploads receipts into QuickBooks," Timothy explained.

He grinned as he added, "But here's where the magic *really* happens—those receipts don't just stop at QuickBooks. They flow through your entire system like water through pipes, from Dext to QuickBooks and all the way over to BuilderTrend. That dusty receipt from the lumberyard that used to sit forgotten in your truck now automatically updates your job costing in real-time. One photo ties everything together, and suddenly everyone knows exactly where each project stands financially—no more surprises when it's too late to do anything about them."

The idea of reducing paperwork and manual data entry was nothing short of revolutionary to me. I could picture my office desk—once cluttered with receipts and scribbled notes—transformed into a clean, digital workspace where every expense was just a click away.

And then there was Bill.com, which rounded out the suite of tools Timothy recommended. "Bill.com is for managing payments," he said, "it ensures that every bill is paid on time. It integrates with QuickBooks Online, so you're not juggling multiple systems. It's like having a personal assistant who never forgets a due date!"

He traced the journey with his finger, like he was mapping a river's path. "Here's what saved my sanity—when a vendor bill arrives, we upload it directly into BuilderTrend where your project manager can review it. Once approved, it automatically flows into QuickBooks for accounting and then posts to Bill.com, just waiting for you to hit that final payment button. One upload, three systems, zero headaches."

As our Zoom call continued, Timothy's voice grew more animated. He was painting a picture of a modern, efficient operation where technology took the chaos out of everyday tasks. "These tools definitely aren't *magic*," he cautioned, "but they're specifically designed to help you make better decisions. They give you data, insights, and a level of control that manual methods simply can't match."

I found myself imagining a day when I could check a dashboard on my computer and see everything from project progress to cash flow, all updated in real time. It was nothing like the old days of piles of paperwork and frantic phone calls. With BuilderTrend, I could manage all my projects in one centralized system. With QuickBooks Online, I could see the financial pulse of my business without the usual delay. Dext would take care of the messy details of expense tracking, and Bill.com would ensure that our relationships with vendors and subcontractors remained strong, thanks to prompt payments.

Timothy's practical advice was all about integrating them into the fabric of the business. "You need to choose the right tools for the size and needs of your company," he said. "Not every tool is a perfect fit for every business. It's about finding what works for you and then committing to it. That means proper setup, training your team on how to use them, and, most importantly, using them consistently."

I remembered how easily things could slip back into chaos if these tools weren't used diligently. There was no shortcut here—the technology was only as good as the process behind it. I took notes, scribbling down action items: set up a training session for BuilderTrend; integrate QuickBooks as our new accounting system; start using Dext to capture every receipt; and set up Bill.com to automate our vendor payments. It was a lot to digest, but the promise of a streamlined operation was too enticing to ignore.

Over the next few weeks, I began the gradual process of adopting these technologies. I started with BuilderTrend, spending an afternoon with one of their support specialists via Zoom. The specialist walked me through creating project timelines, setting up communication channels with clients, and even handling change orders digitally. I was amazed at how intuitive the system was—almost as if it were designed with people like me in mind, people tired of the constant scramble.

Next came QuickBooks Online. I set aside a weekend to migrate our old data into the new system. Thankfully, Timothy was going to join me over a Zoom call to help make sure it was done correct. It wasn't necessarily *easy*—there were many moments of frustration as I reconfigured accounts and verified that every expense was categorized correctly—but the outcome was definitely worth it. I now had a dashboard that gave me a real-time snapshot of our financial health. No more waiting until month's end to get a rough idea of where we stood.

Dext was the tool that practically *reinvented* the way I handled receipts. I remember the first time I snapped a photo of a receipt on my phone, uploaded it, and watched as the software automatically filled in the details. *That* felt like magic—no more sifting through piles of paper or losing track of expenses. Everything was neatly organized and ready for review, which freed up hours of time that I could now devote to more strategic tasks.

Bill.com rounded out the package. Setting it up was surprisingly straightforward. Within a few days, our vendor payments were being managed through the system. I even received notifications on my phone when payments were processed, a small but significant reassurance that our relationships with suppliers were in good hands. It took the worry out of the equation and allowed me to focus on what mattered most: *growing the business.*

Integrating these tools felt like a cultural shift. You could just tell...I began to see the business through a new lens, one where efficiency, transparency, and real-time data were the norms rather than the exceptions. Meetings certainly became more productive; decisions were based on actual numbers rather than gut feelings; and the overall stress level seemed to drop for everyone as the chaos of manual processes gave way to smooth, automated workflows.

I also learned that technology alone isn't enough—it has to be paired with good processes. I worked with my team to develop new standard operating procedures that aligned with these tools. We set up regular training sessions, not just for me but for everyone on the team, to ensure that each person understood how to use the systems effectively. There were moments of resistance, of course—old habits die hard—but gradually, the benefits became undeniable. We began to see fewer mistakes, less rework, and a noticeable improvement in communication across the board.

One afternoon, a few months after we'd fully integrated these tools, I received a message from one of our project managers during a Zoom call. "I just checked BuilderTrend," he said, excitement clear in his voice, "and our project timeline is right on schedule for the first time in months. Everything's tracked, and I know exactly what's coming next." It was a small moment, but it felt monumental.

Timothy's role in all of this was constant, though it was virtual. He would check in with me via Zoom, asking pointed questions about how the tools were working, offering tweaks and advice based on his vast experience. His feedback was always straightforward, sometimes blunt, but always aimed at making sure I wasn't just buying technology for technology's sake. "Remember," he'd say during one call, "the tools are only as good as the processes behind them. Make sure you're using them to solve real problems, not just to impress clients."

Now that we had the right tools in place, it was time to start using them effectively. Because no matter how much technology we had, if we didn't understand what the numbers meant, we were still flying blind. That's where Timothy's next lesson came in—teaching me how to truly read the financial story behind my business.

CHAPTER 12

THE LANGUAGE OF NUMBERS

When Timothy and I first sat down to review the financials, I realized how disconnected I was from the numbers that kept my entire operation afloat. Sure, I knew how much I was paying for materials and roughly how much I was charging clients, but I'd never looked at it as a story—a narrative that reveals where money is wasted, where jobs go off-track, and where the business can actually grow. Timothy, on the other hand, saw numbers as the language of a construction company. If I couldn't speak that language, I'd never truly steer this business to success.

Timothy handed me a P&L from the previous quarter, pointing to a column of figures that looked fine on the surface.

"See this line?" he asked, his voice calm but firm. "It claims you made a profit last month, but did you?"

I shrugged. "That's what it says."

Timothy shook his head. "But look here—some invoices haven't been accounted for, and half your overhead isn't in these totals. This P&L is lying to you because the data's incomplete."

I felt a flush of embarrassment, thinking back to how many times I'd glanced at these numbers and assumed we were "doing okay." I'd always believed that as long as I kept the crew busy and the checks were coming in, the finances would take care of themselves. Timothy wanted to show me that ignorance had been costing me—repeatedly.

He pushed another document forward: a bank statement. "Compare this with your P&L," he said. "If your P&L shows a profit, but your bank account keeps shrinking, something's off."

I scanned the pages, finding something concerning in revenue and expenses. I spotted recurring charges I'd nearly forgotten about—tools I'd financed, monthly software fees, random supply runs. Each one seemed small in isolation, but together they added up. Timothy pointed out that these unplanned expenses were messing up cash flow.

"You've been flying blind," Timothy said, tapping the paper. "Even if you were making a profit on paper, you'd never see that money if you're constantly plugging holes you didn't know existed."

Timothy then slid a credit card statement across the desk. "This is the silent killer for a lot of contractors," he said. "Running short on cash, you swipe your card here and there, thinking you'll pay it off once the next client check comes in. But each interest charge, each unpaid balance, can eat into your margins."

I glanced over the list of transactions: gas for the trucks, last-minute supplies, even a few impulsive buys for the office that I'd rationalized as "necessary." Nothing felt extravagant by itself, but collectively, these small charges explained why I always seemed strapped for cash near the end of every month.

"By the time you notice the debt piling up," Timothy continued, "the interest and fees have already siphoned off what little buffer you had. Then you're one delayed client payment away from a crisis."

After laying out the documents, Timothy began walking me step-by-step through the concept of job costing. "If you don't track every dollar that goes into a job—labor, materials, overhead—you'll have no idea if you're actually earning money," he said. "You might think you're turning a profit, but maybe you're just staying afloat because of a good project or two."

He had me break down a recent kitchen remodel we'd done: everything from the lumber and drywall to the time each carpenter spent. I was shocked at how many expenses I'd never bothered to list, like small hardware runs or the extra day of painting when the client changed the color choice. Timothy called these "hidden costs" that accumulate over the life of a project, sabotaging your profit margin if you don't plan for them.

"Imagine you're cooking a dish," he explained. "You need to know exactly how much of each ingredient goes in, or you can't replicate it—or price it—accurately. Construction's no different. Job costing is your recipe. If you skip steps, the result is inconsistent and probably more expensive than it should be."

It wasn't that I'd never heard of job costing. I'd just always found it tedious to document every nail and hour spent. But Timothy argued that it wasn't optional if I wanted to grow. "Small contractors get away with seat-of-the-pants pricing, but as soon as you take on bigger jobs or multiple projects at once, the confusion multiplies," he said. "Without a clear handle on costs, you might underbid to win a contract, then lose your shirt on labor overruns."

We spent what felt like an eternity reviewing each line item for that kitchen remodel, comparing it to my rough estimate. Sure enough, I'd missed hundreds in small supply runs, and I'd underestimated labor by almost 20% because of a couple of last-minute changes. No wonder I'd ended up frustrated when the final payout seemed smaller than I expected.

Timothy then shifted gears to budgets and cash flow. "Think of your budget as a roadmap," he said. "It's not just about setting a target; it's about forecasting month by month, project by project, so you can see where the shortfalls might happen."

I'd always associated budgets with large corporations or city governments—not my imperfect construction company. But as Timothy pointed out, the unpredictability of construction made budgeting even more critical. If I knew I had two major invoices due in the same week, I could plan to have enough reserves to cover them, or I could reschedule some expenses.

He showed me how to project my cash flow for the next three months, factoring in client payment schedules and the expected costs of ongoing projects. It was eye-opening. I realized that certain months looked flush on paper but actually had big material or labor outlays that would drain the account before a client's final payment arrived. Without planning for that gap, I'd be tempted to rely on credit cards again—or skip paying myself to cover the difference.

"If you keep skipping your own paycheck," Timothy said, pointing at the budget, "you're treating yourself as non-essential. You'll end up resenting the business or making desperate decisions to grab quick cash. Neither is good for sustainability."

Over the next few weeks, I immersed myself in these lessons. I'd start each morning reviewing the previous day's expenses in QuickBooks Online, carefully examining how each transaction was categorized by job and project. What once took hours of manual spreadsheet work now happened with just a few simple clicks, though the discipline of daily review remained absolutely essential.

I'd glance at the bank balance to see if it matched the projected cash flow for that date. Sometimes I found discrepancies—maybe we'd ordered more materials than expected or a client's check cleared a day early—and I'd tweak the budget accordingly. While this manual process was time-consuming, Timothy assured me that we would eventually implement more automated solutions as we continued to improve. As I got more comfortable, I started explaining the basics to my team during weekly meetings. "Here's why filling out timesheets accurately matters," I said one Wednesday. "It's not just paperwork. It tells us how many labor hours a job actually took, so we can bid correctly next time. If we estimate 50 hours and it takes 70, we're losing money."

It was a new conversation for them, too. They were used to hearing me harp on deadlines and clients, but not so much about finances. Yet I noticed they took pride in understanding how their efficiency impacted the bottom line. If they finished a job on schedule, they saw how it boosted our profit. If there were repeated mistakes, they saw the extra labor hours that chewed into our earnings.

Timothy applauded this transparency. "When the crew understands the numbers, they become partners in controlling costs," he said. "They realize it's not just about pleasing the boss; it's about making sure the company stays profitable so everyone keeps working."

That mindset shift was gradual but effective. Carpenters would double-check material lists to avoid unnecessary runs to the supply store. Mark, our site superintendent, kept a closer eye on who was logging overtime and why. Everyone became more conscious of the ripple effect that even small oversights could have.

One day, Mark showed me how he was using the job costing report in BuilderTrend that Timothy had helped us set up. He'd review daily labor hours against the budgeted amount in real-time, giving us immediate visibility into how each project was tracking. If he noticed they were falling behind, he'd figure out why: was there an unexpected snag, or was someone just not pulling their weight? By catching these issues early, he prevented cost overruns that previously blindsided us at the project's end.

Timothy also coached me on reading the P&L more critically. "Don't just look at that bottom line," he warned. "Dig into the revenue sources, the categories of expenses, and see if something's spiking unexpectedly." He showed me how overhead costs—like insurance, office rent, and utilities—could balloon if I wasn't careful. He also cautioned me to pay attention to "cost of goods sold" on the profit and loss statement, which included materials, subcontractors, and labor.

"Overhead is the silent killer," he said. "If you don't keep it proportionate to your revenue, you'll find yourself needing bigger and bigger jobs just to stay afloat."

Seeing the numbers plainly made me more disciplined. I postponed buying certain tools until I knew we had enough projects lined up to justify them. I consolidated software subscriptions, canceling ones we rarely used. The savings weren't dramatic individually, but they added up, freeing capital to invest in areas that genuinely boosted productivity—like updated safety gear.

Timothy also helped me refine how I tracked expenses for each project. Before, I'd lump them all into one big category labeled "materials." Now, I broke them down: lumber, drywall, electrical, plumbing, etc. That granularity let me see which materials were driving up costs and whether certain jobs needed more precise estimates. It also made me aware of potential waste. If I noticed we were consistently overspending on a specific type of material, I'd investigate: were we ordering too much? Was a supplier charging too high a rate?

One of the most empowering things about learning this "language of numbers" was the ability to make data-driven decisions about which projects to take. In the past, if a new job sounded big and impressive, I'd jump on it—only to realize later the margins were thin or the client was a slow payer. Now, I'd do a quick forecast: how many labor hours did we expect? What were the material costs? Did the client have a solid payment record? If the numbers didn't pencil out, I'd either negotiate the contract or walk away.

That might have seemed risky—turning down projects—but Timothy reminded me that doing the wrong job can be worse than doing no job. "Better to do fewer, high-quality projects with solid margins than scramble through a dozen that barely cover expenses," he said. "Taking on project with better margins will increase cash flow and allow you to put money in reserves so that you don't have to rush into another project right away. Wouldn't that be nice?"

In the months that followed, I noticed a tangible difference in my stress levels. No longer did I go into a mild panic every time payroll was due, uncertain if the bank account could handle it. I had a schedule of incoming checks, a budget for each major bill, and a small cushion for emergencies. I wasn't flush with cash by any means, but I wasn't lurching from one crisis to another.

There was a particular moment when we wrapped up a sizable remodel and the final numbers came in almost exactly as we projected—a mere 2% variance. Normally, I might have brushed that off as a happy coincidence. But Timothy made a point of highlighting it. "That's what solid job costing and budgeting does for you," he said. "You didn't rely on guesswork, and you didn't let hidden costs go unnoticed."

That remodel also finished on time, giving us a happy client who left a glowing review. Best of all, I went into the next project with confidence because the data confirmed we could handle the schedule and the costs. If I saw a snag, I had the tools to adjust early.

I also started holding brief monthly finance reviews with my core staff. We'd put key figures on a whiteboard: total revenue, expenses, current overhead, and labor hours for the major projects. I'd explain that if we stayed within budget on each job, we'd maintain decent profit margins. If we saw any category spiking (maybe we were running too much overtime), we discussed solutions before it spiraled. In a way, these reviews helped everyone feel accountable—nobody wanted to be the reason the margin dipped that month.

Timothy warned me not to get complacent just because I'd learned the basics. "Numbers change, the market changes, your overhead changes," he said. "Keep refining. Keep verifying."

He emphasized regular reconciliations: matching the bank statements, credit card statements, and P&L every month to ensure we weren't carrying hidden discrepancies forward. I wasn't going to lie—it was tedious sometimes. But the payoff was huge. I finally knew, day by day, where the business stood financially. That knowledge informed every decision: from what subcontractors to use, to whether we had enough surplus to invest in a new piece of equipment, to how aggressively we could bid on an upcoming project.

One of my proudest moments came when a local developer approached me about a massive commercial build. In the old days, I'd have jumped at the chance, thrown out a rough bid, and hoped for the best. This time, I invited him to talk specifics. Then I spent a weekend meticulously costing out labor, materials, overhead, and contingencies. By Monday, I had a solid estimate that accounted for likely delays, a realistic profit margin, and enough buffer to handle minor surprises.

When he saw the proposal, he commented on how detailed my breakdown was compared to other contractors he'd worked with. It wasn't just a random total with disclaimers—it was a line-by-line narrative of how we'd get to the finish line. He respected that level of clarity, and we ended up signing the contract.

Timothy gave me a nod of approval when I told him. "That's the power of numbers," he said. "They don't just protect you from losses; they give you credibility. Clients see you're not bluffing."

At our last monthly review, I stood at the head of the table, pointing to a graph that showed how our job costing accuracy had improved by 30% over the past six months. The team smiled, maybe a bit relieved that all those timesheets and cost reports were paying off. "This is your doing," I told them. "Every time you fill out a timecard properly or track a material purchase, you're giving us the data we need to steer this ship."

It felt good to say that. Because the language of numbers isn't just something for me and Timothy to parse—it's a conversation that everyone in the company can contribute to. Once they realize their daily actions shape the bottom line, they take ownership.

Stepping out of that meeting, I thought about how different life used to be before Timothy made me face the numbers head-on. I'd dreaded looking at the bank account, worried about what I'd find. Now, I check it with curiosity, thinking, "What's the next move?"

Chapter 13

What Key Performance Indicators Matter?

I remember a drizzly Tuesday morning when I logged into our weekly Zoom call with Timothy. We'd been talking for months about the numbers—cash flow, job costing, and overhead—but he had a certain gleam in his eye that told me we were stepping onto new ground.

"Let me share my screen with you," Timothy said, clicking a few buttons. His face minimized to the corner as his desktop came into view. I watched as he navigated through several folders and opened a familiar Profit and Loss statement. The document filled my screen, with Timothy's cursor hovering over specific sections.

"Look at these figures," he said, using his cursor to highlight key lines on the digital report. "They're decent, but they don't tell you the whole story. Not every number matters equally. If you don't know where to focus, you can get lost in the noise."

I glanced over the P&L on my own screen, thinking that it was already giving me a good picture of how we stood. We had some revenue, some expenses, and a line showing profit—or at least something that *claimed* to be profit. But Timothy insisted that the truly revealing data wasn't just in the final totals; it was in specific metrics that could expose the strengths and weaknesses of my operation.

He called them Key Performance Indicators, or KPIs. "You've probably heard the term," he said. "But I want you to see how each one relates to your construction business. If you track them carefully, they become an early warning system and a guide to better decisions."

"Now let's look at something different," Timothy said, clicking to open a new document on his screen. "This is your job costing budget report, which gives us information we can't see on the Profit and Loss statement."

He gestured with his cursor across the detailed spreadsheet showing individual projects, their budgeted costs, actual expenses, and resulting margins.

"See, while the P&L gives you an overall picture of your business performance, it won't break down profits by individual project. That's why we need this job costing report to *really* understand what's happening," Timothy explained. "Without this level of detail, you might think your business is doing fine based on the P&L alone, but you wouldn't see which specific projects are dragging you down."

After I'd had a moment to absorb the difference between the two reports, Timothy continued.

"Start with profit margins," he said, highlighting a column of percentages on the job costing report. "It's basic, but it matters. You look at your overall profit margin on the P&L, but also your profit margin on each project right here. That's where you see if your pricing is realistic."

I nodded. I'd seen times where the books claimed we were making money, but somehow, I was always short at the end of the month. Timothy flipped to a page highlighting a gross profit margin in a recent quarter on the P&L. It looked acceptable, but he pointed out that it was inflated by one large project that happened to go smoothly.

"This is exactly why we need both reports," he said, gesturing between the P&L and the job costing budget report. "On the P&L, your overall numbers look fine. But when we check the job costing report..." he switched back to the detailed project view, "...we can see that a couple of other projects actually lost money, dragging down your real average. Without this detailed breakdown, you'd never know which jobs are actually profitable."

"You can't just look at the overall number," he said, "you have to break it down by job. If one project is covering the losses on two others, that's not sustainable."

Timothy's second KPI was Direct Labor Efficiency Ratio. "Construction is labor-intensive," he said. "If your crew wastes hours on rework or disorganized tasks, you're losing money every minute they stand around or fix mistakes."

This one hit home. I'd lost count of the times my crew took longer than planned because someone forgot to order the right materials, or a client changed a detail at the last second. Or because I had an inexperienced worker who needed constant supervision. Timothy suggested I calculate labor efficiency by calculating this ratio with actual labor costs and estimated labor costs for each phase of a job.

"If you find that this ratio is trending down to zero," he said, "that's a red flag. Are you underestimating to make the bid more attractive, or are the crews underperforming? Either way, you need to figure it out."

I recalled a recent remodel where we'd run two weeks behind schedule. Mark insisted the job was standard, but halfway through, the office manager admitted he hadn't scheduled the drywall delivery properly. The crew spent days waiting or doing busywork while I scrambled to get materials in place. That inefficiency didn't just affect our timeline—it ate into profits because we had to pay the crew for days they weren't fully productive. If I'd tracked labor efficiency from the start, I might have caught the lag sooner.

Equipment Utilization Percentage was Timothy's third KPI. "This industry runs on heavy machinery—skid steers, excavators, trucks. But if your gear sits idle, you're paying for it without getting a return."

I'd been there before. I recalled a fancy piece of equipment I purchased for a big commercial job. We finished the main excavation in half the expected time, which was great, but the machine then sat around for another week because our schedule was off, and we couldn't return it early without penalty. We hardly touched it. That's money straight out of my pocket.

Timothy leaned forward. "Ask yourself: how much time do these machines spend actually working? How often are they rented out to other crews, or do they just gather dust on your lot? Track that percentage. If it's low, maybe you should rent equipment on an as-needed basis or sell something you're not using."

Fourth on Timothy's list was overhead ratio. He described overhead as the silent killer, and I believed him. I'd seen overhead creep up slowly—office rent, software subscriptions, marketing costs—until it weighed us down. It wasn't like materials or labor that we could pin directly to a single job. It was a constant drain that needed steady revenue to cover.

"Keep your overhead ratio in check," Timothy said. "If overhead is too high a percentage of your revenue, you end up struggling to turn a profit. And if revenue dips, that overhead can bury you."

He opened a chart that tracked our overhead for the past year, comparing it to monthly income. I cringed at the upward slope. "When times were good, you spent on extra staff, bigger office space, and new gadgets," Timothy pointed out. "Then a slowdown hit, but your overhead remained high. You had to burn through cash or rely on credit."

He was right. I'd seen how one slow month triggered a chain reaction: I'd scramble to pay basic bills, my credit card balance would balloon, and I'd end up cutting corners on projects to stay afloat. That overhead ratio spelled out exactly why.

The remarkable thing was how all these KPIs worked together. Timothy showed me how an excellent profit margin could be undone by poor labor efficiency, or how good labor efficiency might still fail to yield profits if my overhead was too heavy. It was like looking at a puzzle—each piece a vital indicator of the company's well-being. If any piece lagged, the entire puzzle was off.

We spent the rest of that drizzly Tuesday identifying which KPIs were most relevant to my particular business model. Some contractors might emphasize one set of metrics over another, but Timothy urged me to track them all, at least to start. "Later, you can fine-tune which ones to focus on," he said, "but don't ignore a KPI just because it's not as flashy. Sometimes the smallest data points reveal the biggest problems."

I walked away with a list: profit margin by project, direct labor efficiency ratio, equipment utilization percentage, and overhead ratio. Timothy also suggested a few others—like NCE (Net Cash Exposure) or D/E (Debt-to-Equity Ratio)—but we agreed to tackle the core four first.

Implementing this new KPI mindset felt daunting. I started by teaching my foremen and office staff what these metrics meant in simple terms. "When we talk about labor efficiency," I explained at a weekly meeting, "we're looking at how much labor cost versus how much labor cost we budgeted. If we overshoot every time, we're either estimating poorly or wasting time on the job site."

The crew responded more positively than I'd expected. Many of them were tired of hearing me complain about running late or over budget without giving them concrete benchmarks. Now, they had measurable goals: keep labor cost within 10% of the estimate, aim for at least 80% equipment usage on each job, and maintain overhead below a certain percentage of revenue each month.

I started building a simple dashboard on my laptop using spreadsheets, meticulously tracking data from BuilderTrend Job Costing Budget Report. Every morning, I'd glance at it to see if anything was flashing red. If labor hours spiked on a certain job, I'd call the foreman. If overhead inched up too high, I'd investigate whether we'd made a big purchase or added a recurring expense we could have postponed. If equipment sat idle for more than a couple of days, I'd ask Mark, our site superintendent, whether we should rent it out or move it to a project that actually needed it.

One day, around a month into this KPI-driven approach, I noticed the equipment utilization percentage dipped alarmingly low on a major site. We had an expensive crane sitting idle because the steel delivery was delayed. In the past, I might have shrugged this off as hitting a rough patch, but now I saw it for what it was: a daily drain on the budget. We called the supplier to push for an earlier delivery window, explaining the cost implications. Even a single day's improvement helped. We also arranged a quick side job to use the crane for a smaller project down the road, which at least offset some of the cost.

That kind of proactive response became more frequent as we tracked each KPI. Instead of letting wasted time fester, we pounced on solutions. Instead of complaining that overhead was suffocating us, we systematically shaved off unnecessary expenses when we saw the ratio creeping upward.

One afternoon, Timothy called to check on our progress. "How's the KPI approach treating you?" he asked.

I told him about the crane incident and how we'd diverted it to another job. "Honestly, this is a game-changer," I admitted. "Before, I would've just accepted the delay, telling myself that's how construction goes. Now, I see the numbers, and it lights a fire under me to fix the problem."

Timothy sounded pleased. "That's exactly what KPIs do," he said. "They replace vague guesswork with real data, so you can adapt quickly. If a metric flags a problem, you address it right away instead of discovering it too late."

We also began setting specific targets for each KPI:

• Profit margin: Aim for at least 40% on each job.

• Direct labor efficiency ratio: Keep the ratio at a 4 or better.

• Equipment utilization: 70–80% usage minimum, or we reconsider renting.

• Overhead ratio: Keep overhead under 30% of revenue each month.

Of course, these targets weren't set in stone. Some high-end projects could allow for a bigger margin, while a quick fix-up might settle for less. Sometimes overhead spiked if we invested in new software or took on a large marketing push. But having a baseline gave us a yardstick to measure progress.

With these KPIs guiding our day-to-day, I saw a ripple effect across the company. My foremen started double-checking the labor hours they bid, pushing back on me if I suggested an unrealistic schedule. Maria, our bookkeeper, kept a closer eye on overhead expenses, emailing me whenever she saw a new subscription or a spike in utility bills. Mark kept a utilization calendar for our major equipment, planning out exactly where each machine would go and for how long.

Clients started noticing, too. Our bids became tighter, with fewer surprises mid-project because we'd done a thorough job-cost analysis upfront. We often finished projects closer to the estimated timeline, which improved our reputation. And when a delay did occur, the team spotted it early and found workarounds, saving time overall.

It wasn't always perfect. Sometimes the overhead ratio jumped if we had a slow month, or direct labor efficiency dipped because we overstaffed three projects. But at least we knew what was happening and could respond. If we saw direct labor efficiency dropping on one job, we'd investigate: Did we miscalculate, or was the crew lacking direction? If it was a miscalculation, we'd learn for next time. If it was a crew issue, we'd fix it now—maybe send an extra supervisor or clarify responsibilities.

Timothy loved hearing these little success stories. He'd grin whenever I recounted how a site superintendent caught a budget overrun a week before it spiraled out of control. "KPIs aren't just numbers," he kept saying. "They're the heartbeat of your operation. Listen to them, and you'll spot the warning signs before the patient goes critical."

One day, after we'd wrapped a commercial renovation with better-than-expected margins, I pulled Timothy aside. "I finally get it," I said, "the difference between glancing at a Profit and Loss statement and truly tracking KPIs. The P&L is just a snapshot. KPIs show you the trends, the weak spots, and where you can improve."

He nodded. "Exactly. A P&L might tell you last month's results, but a KPI can show you real-time performance. If your direct labor efficiency is sliding this week, you can fix it before it sinks the entire project."

The more comfortable I got with these metrics, the more I realized we could refine them to suit our unique situation. For instance, we broke down direct labor efficiency by trade—carpenters vs. electricians vs. painters. That let us see which trade was consistently behind schedule. If overhead soared one month, we pinpointed whether it was a big marketing investment or just too many minor expenses adding up.

Eventually, we introduced a couple of additional KPIs that Timothy suggested:

• **Change Order Frequency:** How often do clients request change orders, and how do those changes affect labor hours and profit?

• **Schedule Variance:** How closely do we stick to the planned timeline for each project?

Both gave us more insight into potential pitfalls. If we noticed a project with frequent change orders, we'd ask ourselves if we were scoping the job poorly at the start. If schedule variance kept growing, we'd examine whether we were underestimating complexities or if the crew wasn't on the same page.

I began to see that focusing on these metrics was less about policing everyone and more about creating a culture of accountability and improvement. The team felt motivated to hit those labor hour targets and keep equipment busy because they understood it benefited all of us. It was no longer me nagging about budgets—everyone had a stake.

One afternoon, a site foreman showed me the daily log he was maintaining. He'd note exactly how many crew members worked each day, which tasks they completed, and if they ran into any blockers. Then he'd compare that log to our labor estimate. If they ended up two hours behind, he'd flag the reason: maybe a piece of equipment broke, or a last-minute change required a trip to the supply store. That level of detail fed directly into our direct labor efficiency metric, giving us a near-real-time pulse on whether we were on track.

Of course, it wasn't all smooth sailing. We hit snags—a crane breakdown that skewed our equipment utilization for a week, an uptick in overhead when we decided to invest in new project management software, and some blowouts on labor when a client decided to rip out an entire floor at the last minute. But each time, we measured the impact and made adjustments with eyes wide open, rather than being blindsided at the end of the job.

Looking back, it astonishes me how I used to run the company largely on gut feelings. I'd sense that a project was going well or poorly without having solid data to back it up. If profits dipped, I'd blame external factors or assume the next job would balance the books. Now, with KPIs at the center of my decision-making, I can't imagine going back to that haphazard approach.

At a recent all-hands meeting, I decided to share how each KPI had improved over the last quarter. Profit margins were up because we bid jobs more accurately and managed costs. Direct labor efficiency ratio had inched closer to our target, thanks to better planning and communication. Equipment utilization percentage was at its highest since we started tracking, partly because we sold off one underused bulldozer and rented more strategically. Overhead ratio had finally plateaued, meaning we weren't drowning in monthly bills. It felt good to show the team their hard work had tangible results.

After that meeting, one of the younger carpenters pulled me aside. "You know, I never thought about numbers in construction—figured it was all about building stuff. But seeing those graphs made me realize why we do things the way we do."

I smiled. That was precisely Timothy's point: once people see how their daily actions reflect in the KPIs, they take ownership. It's not just the owner's problem anymore; it's everyone's job to keep the dials in the right zone.

Timothy dropped by the office the next day, and I walked him through the dashboard. He raised an eyebrow at how organized it was. "You sure this is the same person who used to avoid spreadsheets?" he joked.

I laughed, remembering my old habit of stuffing invoices into drawers. "Hey, people change," I said. "Especially when they see the difference real metrics can make."

He gave me that approving nod I'd grown to appreciate. "Just don't forget: KPIs will evolve as your business does. Keep them relevant, keep them updated. And always be ready to adapt when the data tells you something new."

Chapter 14

Are the KPIs Telling the Truth?

One early morning, I logged into Zoom with a cup of lukewarm coffee in hand. I wasn't sure what to expect—these virtual meetings with Timothy had become a sort of ritual by now—but I knew that today's session was going to be different. Today, we were going to dive deep into our KPIs.

On the screen, Timothy's face appeared, framed by his neatly arranged home office. He gave a small nod and said, "Good morning. Today, I want to talk about something that's been gnawing at you for a while: Are your KPIs really telling you the truth?"

I paused for a moment, thinking back on all the frantic nights I'd spent poring over spreadsheets, trying to decipher rows and rows of numbers that never quite added up in my mind. "To be honest, I always thought big numbers were my safety net," I admitted. "I trusted them to tell me what's working and what isn't. But sometimes... I feel like I'm missing something."

Timothy leaned forward. "Well, numbers don't lie, but they can be misleading if you don't know how to read them correctly. It's not enough to just track them; you need to understand what they mean in the context of your business."

He began by pointing to a detailed KPI dashboard he had shared on his screen—a colorful array of graphs and charts that looked more like a modern art piece than the financial health of my company. "Take your profit margins, for instance," he said. "They're critical, but if you're only looking at them in isolation, you might miss underlying issues. You have to look at them alongside direct labor efficiency, equipment utilization, and overhead ratios."

I frowned, trying to recall the last time I'd cross-referenced those numbers. "Sometimes I get caught up in short-term fluctuations," I confessed. "A dip in profit margins one month would send me into a panic, even though I knew it might just be a temporary setback. But then I'd see a spike the next month, and it would feel like a win. How do I know what's a real trend versus just a blip?"

Timothy smiled slightly, as if he'd been waiting for me to ask that very question. "That's exactly what I'm here to help with," he said. "Let's break it down. Short-term fluctuations are like the waves on the ocean—they're constantly moving, sometimes high, sometimes low. But what really matters is the tide—the long-term trend. You need to track your KPIs over a period of time, say, six to twelve months, to understand the real direction of your business."

He then shared a few examples from his own experience. "For instance," he explained, "I once worked with a contractor who would panic every time his weekly profit margin dipped by just a few percentage points. But once we mapped out his data over a full year, we saw that the fluctuations were just seasonal variations. What really mattered was that, overall, his margin was improving steadily. That's the kind of insight you need to cultivate."

I scribbled notes as Timothy's words resonated with me. I began to realize that I had been too reactive—too focused on the day-to-day numbers—without taking the time to see the bigger picture. "So, you're saying I need to set up some sort of baseline for each KPI?" I asked.

"Exactly," Timothy replied. "Establish a benchmark that represents your business at its best. Then, measure every month against that benchmark. If you see a consistent deviation, that's a sign something's off." He paused, letting the advice sink in. "But be careful—don't overreact to a single outlier. One bad month doesn't mean the system is broken. It's the pattern over time that matters."

I took a deep breath and remembered the seemingly countless nights spent agonizing over minor details, wondering if I'd made a fatal error. In hindsight, many of those sleepless hours were just wasted energy. I'd been so busy reacting to every little shift that I'd lost sight of the long-term trends.

Timothy's next point hit home. "Another common mistake is focusing on the wrong metrics," he said. "For example, you might obsess over how many projects you've completed, but if you're not measuring the profitability of those projects, you're missing the point. You need to ask yourself: Are these projects driving growth, or are they just adding to the workload without real returns?"

I nodded, recalling several projects where I'd been proud of the volume of work but later discovered that the margins were terrible—expenses had ballooned, and labor inefficiencies had eaten into every dollar of profit. "I've seen that happen," I admitted. "I'd get excited about the new contracts and then, months later, realize that they weren't really beneficial at all."

Timothy leaned back in his chair. "It's all about balance. When you're setting KPIs, prioritize the ones that directly impact your bottom line. Profit margins, direct labor efficiency ratio, equipment utilization percentage—these are your core metrics. Overhead ratios, while important, should be looked at in context. And don't forget about cash flow. If you can't pay your bills on time, no amount of profit on paper means anything."

The conversation turned practical. Timothy walked me through how to build a simple dashboard—a digital tool that consolidated all the key KPIs in one place. He demonstrated, via screen-share, how to set up graphs that showed trends over time. "See this line graph?" he said, pointing to a steadily climbing curve. "That's your profit margin over the last year. And here's a bar chart for direct labor efficiency ratio. When you see these two in tandem, you can start to correlate dips and spikes."

He also showed me how to use filters and comparisons. "If you're looking at a spike in equipment downtime, don't just assume it's because of poor management," he advised. "Check the context: Was there a major repair that month forcing the equipment to sit idle? Did you have a temporary lull between projects? Was the equipment awaiting specialized parts that were delayed in shipping? Understanding the 'why' behind the numbers is crucial."

I felt a growing sense of empowerment as the data began to make sense. For the first time, I was *interpreting* the numbers. I realized that each KPI was a piece of a puzzle that, when assembled correctly, painted a clear picture of the business's health.

The conversation shifted to common pitfalls. Timothy cautioned me against the tendency to chase every new metric that came along. "There's a temptation in today's digital age to track every conceivable data point," he said. "But not all of them are relevant. You need to focus on the metrics that matter most for your specific business model. Otherwise, you're just drowning in data."

He shared a story about another contractor who had implemented a vast array of KPIs—so many, in fact, that he couldn't keep track of them all. "That guy was trying to measure everything," Timothy recalled, "and in the end, nothing got measured properly. You have to be selective. Start with the essentials, get those right, and then add more only if they provide additional insight."

I jotted down a few key points on my notepad:

- **Profit Margins**: The heart of project viability.
- **Direct Labor Efficiency Ratio**: Measure's the crew's performance in relation to job profit.
- **Equipment Utilization Percentage**: Ensuring every machine is a profit center.
- **Overhead Ratios**: Keeping fixed costs in check.
- **Cash Flow**: The lifeblood of daily operations.

As we talked, I began to recognize the patterns that were emerging within my own business data. I realized that while my profit margins sometimes looked good on a monthly basis, there were underlying issues with the direct labor efficiency ratio that, over time, were eating into my success. I could correlate dips in efficiency with specific projects where poor planning had led to overtime hours and rework. Equipment utilization percentage was another area that had been a blind spot—if a piece of machinery sat idle for too long, it was a drain on resources that could tip a project from profitable to loss-making.

Timothy emphasized the importance of *context*. "Short-term fluctuations are natural," he said. "A single month's dip in profit margins isn't a disaster if the overall trend is upward. But if you see that dip repeating month after month, that's a warning sign." He explained that it was the long-term trends, the patterns over several months, that provided the true picture. "Learn to read between the lines," he added. "Understand that every number is part of a larger narrative."

I began to feel a sense of clarity that had eluded me for so long. The next few weeks were a period of intense analysis and recalibration. I restructured our reporting system so that key KPIs were updated weekly rather than daily. I started having a short Zoom call with my strategic advisor every Friday to go over the numbers, a routine that became as essential as my morning coffee. These sessions became about anticipating problems before they became crises.

One Friday, after a particularly enlightening call, I realized that I had begun to trust the numbers in a way I never had before. I could see, *clearly*, the relationship between increased direct labor efficiency ratio and improved profit margins, or how a slight uptick in equipment downtime forecasted a spike in overhead costs. I started making decisions with a new kind of confidence, knowing that the data wasn't just an afterthought—it was a guide.

The more I engaged with the KPIs, the more I started sharing insights with my team. In our weekly team Zoom meetings, I'd highlight a few key charts and graphs, pointing out trends and discussing what they meant for our operations. It began to feel like storytelling! "Last month, our direct labor efficiency ratio dropped by 5%," I'd say, "and that directly translated to increased overtime and reduced profit margins. Here's what we can do to get back on track." It was about creating a culture where everyone understood that their work had a measurable impact on the business.

These meetings sometimes sparked wonderful discussions, with crew members offering suggestions based on their day-to-day experiences. One project manager once noted, "I've seen that when we start a project with a clear set of targets, the team works faster and with fewer mistakes." That comment, simple as it was, underscored a crucial point: numbers, when understood correctly, could drive better performance and even improve morale.

In one of our later Zoom sessions, Timothy summarized it perfectly. "KPIs are your business's pulse," he said. "They tell you when something's off—when a project is heading into the red or when your operations are running too hot. But they can only do that if you're paying attention."

CHAPTER 15

PAYING YOURSELF FIRST

One day it hit me like a ton of bricks—the day I realized that in trying to keep the business afloat, I'd completely forgotten to take care of *myself*. I'd been so consumed with the endless hustle of meeting deadlines, patching up mistakes, and chasing overdue invoices that the concept of paying myself was a foreign one. Then came a Zoom call with Timothy—his familiar, reassuring face filling the screen—and he didn't waste a minute getting straight to the point.

"Listen," Timothy said, his tone calm but unmistakably serious, "if you don't pay yourself first, you're not just undervaluing your own work; you're setting a precedent that could end up costing you more than you ever imagined." I paused, letting his words sink in. For years, I had treated every dollar I earned as if it were meant to be reinvested back into the company, never leaving enough to cover my own basic needs. I'd thought that if I kept pouring money back into the business, eventually it would all pay off. But the truth was, I was bleeding myself dry—both financially and emotionally.

Timothy's approach was never sugarcoated. "You have to figure out your bare minimum," he explained during our virtual meeting, his eyes intense behind his webcam. "Figure out what you need to cover your household expenses—rent, utilities, groceries, everything. That's a *necessity*." I remember feeling a twinge of embarrassment as I admitted that I'd been so focused on keeping the company running that I'd often skipped meals or delayed paying my own bills. It was like I'd been running on fumes, convinced that sacrificing my own well-being was a badge of honor.

He continued, "As an owner-employee of an S or C corporation, you're required by the IRS to pay yourself a reasonable salary. It's a safeguard. It ensures you're not hiding behind your business to avoid personal accountability." I frowned, recalling, once again, the long nights spent agonizing over bank statements and wondering where all the money had gone. That particular realization was painful: I'd been neglecting the one person who mattered most in the business—*myself*.

We dove right into the numbers. Timothy walked me through a rough calculation. "Start by listing your fixed household expenses," he instructed. "Rent or mortgage, utilities, insurance, food, transportation. Add a little extra for emergencies. That's the bare minimum you need to live. Then, consider what a fair salary would be if someone else were doing your job. This is all about acknowledging the value of your expertise." I scrambled to jot down figures, feeling a mix of nervousness and relief as I calculated the minimum amount that would allow me to live without constantly worrying.

Paying yourself is a recognition of the fact that you're the linchpin of the business. When you undervalue yourself, you send a message to your employees that your work, your leadership, isn't worth much. And if that happens, it trickles down to every corner of the company. Timothy made it clear: "When you pay yourself a fair salary, you're saying, 'I'm worth this much, and so is the work we do.' It's a form of self-respect and a cornerstone of sustainable growth."

I recall a Zoom session where Timothy shared a story about another contractor who had struggled with the same issue. This guy, he said, was so stubborn about reinvesting every dollar back into the business that he ended up constantly in financial distress. Not only was his personal life in shambles—missed birthdays, constant stress—but the business suffered as well, because he was too busy worrying about his personal finances to focus on strategy and growth. "Don't be that guy," Timothy warned. "Your business needs you at your best. And you can't be at your best if you're running on empty."

That conversation forced me to reexamine my priorities. I began to see that paying myself was an investment in my own well-being and, by extension, in the health of the business. With Gusto already set up as our payroll solution from our earlier technology implementation, I finally took the step I'd been avoiding—adding myself to the payroll system as a regular employee with a consistent salary. The first official paycheck I received through our automated system was a sweet mix of relief and disbelief. This truly felt like a statement that I *mattered*, that my time and expertise were actually *valuable*.

Timothy was there every step of the way, offering practical tips and a dose of tough love. "You need to balance your personal needs with the business's financial health," he said during one of our Zoom calls. "It's all about ensuring you have enough to function at your best. If you're stressed, if you're constantly worried about how you're going to pay your bills, that anxiety will seep into every decision you make for the business."

I remember the first time I calculated my salary based on actual household expenses. I sat at my kitchen table one night, papers spread out, calculator in hand, and for the first time in years, I felt a tinge of hope that maybe I could have a little peace of mind. I totaled up my monthly expenses—rent, utilities, food, and even a little extra for unexpected costs. The number wasn't astronomical, but it was enough to cover the basics and then some. I set that as my minimum salary and adjusted it upward based on what I believed my role was worth in the market. The process was eye-opening. It forced me to confront not just my financial habits, but my very sense of self-worth.

As I began to pay myself a consistent salary, I noticed some very subtle changes. I started waking up with a little less dread. I could focus on the business without the nagging worry about whether I'd be able to cover the mortgage. My conversations with employees shifted, too! I was no longer the owner who was always scrimping and saving; I was a leader who recognized his value and, by doing so, inspired others to take their roles seriously as well. It wasn't long before I saw the ripple effect: employees began to demand the same level of professionalism and accountability, and it created an environment where everyone felt they were part of a sustainable operation.

There were challenges, of course. Adjusting to the new system wasn't easy, and there were times when I questioned if I was being too hard on myself—or too *lenient* on the business. The balance was a delicate one. I had to ensure that my salary was reasonable in the eyes of the IRS, that it wasn't seen as a way to siphon off profits, but rather as a genuine reflection of the work I was doing. Timothy spent time walking me through the IRS guidelines, explaining what constituted "reasonable compensation" for an owner-employee of an S or C corporation. It was a bureaucratic maze, but it was necessary to ensure that the business remained compliant and that I wasn't putting myself at risk of audits or penalties.

In one memorable Zoom session, Timothy shared a practical tip that I haven't forgotten. "Always look at it this way," he said, leaning in with that piercing gaze of his. "Your salary isn't *just* an expense—it's truly an investment in your own leadership. When you pay yourself, you're funding the very vision that drives this company forward. It sets a standard for everyone else."

I also learned to view my salary in the context of the company's overall financial health. There were quarters when profits were high and I could afford to give myself a bonus, and quarters when the business was not profitable and I couldn't give myself a bonus.

I established a consistent salary that I could maintain throughout the entire year—a baseline that provided stability for both my personal finances and the business. This wasn't a number I'd frequently adjust on a whim. Instead, I approached my compensation with strategic patience, only considering an increase to my base salary when we had clear evidence of sustained growth—when our revenue had not just spiked temporarily but had genuinely matured to a new level that would be maintained going forward. For shorter-term successes, quarterly bonuses became the appropriate way to share in the company's profitable periods without committing to permanent salary increases that might become unsustainable.

What once kept me up at night—figuring out how much I could *safely* pay myself—now gave me a sense of control I'd never experienced before! I could *finally* look at my personal bank account without that knot in my stomach, knowing my business wasn't just surviving, but actually giving both of us room to grow.

One of the more unexpected benefits of paying myself first was the impact it had on my own mindset. I began to see the business differently—not as a relentless money pit, but as a *partnership*—a collaboration between my own personal drive and the collective efforts of my team. With a steady salary, I was less focused on short-term fixes and more on long-term strategies. I could finally invest in training, in upgrading equipment, and in growing the company without the constant fear that I was sacrificing my own stability.

There were moments, especially in the early days of this new approach, when I'd catch myself wondering if I was being too self-indulgent. But then I'd recall a Zoom call with Timothy, where he said, "If you're not paying yourself, you're not really in charge. You're just a COGS (Cost of Goods Sold) in your own machine. Leadership isn't about self-sacrifice to the point of self-destruction. It's about setting boundaries, about recognizing that your own health and well-being are integral to the success of the whole operation."

CHAPTER 16

PAYROLL AND PAYING ON TIME

I'll never forget the moment when the full importance of payroll management *truly* clicked for me—an honest wake-up call delivered during another Zoom call with Timothy. Despite having already implemented Gusto months ago as part of our technology stack, I hadn't *fully* embraced the deeper significance of timely payments. As Timothy's calm, confident face filled my screen that morning, he drove home a point I hadn't fully internalized: *consistent payroll is the foundation of trust and morale.*

"You've got the tool in place with Gusto, but I want to make sure you understand why this matters so much," Timothy said. "Paying your team on time isn't optional. It's the cornerstone of every relationship in your business." Though I'd heard similar statements before, this time it resonated differently. I thought back to those dark days before Gusto, when payroll delays led to frustrated phone calls and plummeting morale. Workers who once arrived with pride began wearing their exhaustion like a badge of defeat. I had dismissed those periods as temporary setbacks—but Timothy helped me confront the reality: when you don't pay people on time, you're not just hurting their bank accounts, you're eroding the very foundation of trust that holds your operation together.

As he spoke, Timothy shared his screen to review our latest Gusto payroll reports. "Let's look at how you can extract even more value from the system you've already implemented," he said, clicking through various dashboards and reports. "The data here gives you insights into labor costs by project, overtime trends, and tax liabilities."

I watched attentively as he demonstrated advanced features I hadn't fully utilized. The system was certainly more powerful than I'd realized. Though we'd been using Gusto for basic payroll processing, I hadn't explored its reporting capabilities or integration potential with our other systems.

I still cringed remembering the pre-Gusto days—particularly one stressful month when a delayed payroll had led to a cascade of problems. We'd been juggling overdue invoices and unexpected project costs, and when payday arrived, the funds simply *weren't there*. I spent that day fielding angry calls and watching morale plummet. The memory stung deeply because it wasn't just about money; it was about respect. When you pay people on time, you're showing that you value their work. When you don't, you're sending the message that they're replaceable parts in a machine that barely cares.

During our call, I reflected on how much Gusto had already transformed our operations in the months since implementation. What had initially seemed intimidating during setup had become second nature. The consultant who helped us link our bank account, sync with QuickBooks, and customize schedules had made the process surprisingly straightforward. The system that had replaced our chaotic mix of manual entries and frantic calculations was now running smoothly in the background of our operations.

"What's particularly valuable about Gusto," Timothy continued, "is how it makes compliance effortless. It generates all necessary tax forms, files them automatically, and provides a complete audit trail. That's a safeguard many construction businesses overlook until they're facing penalties."

Timothy's insights helped me see our payroll system with fresh eyes. "Now that you've got Gusto running smoothly," he said, "remember that payroll isn't just about the mechanics of getting money into people's accounts. It's about establishing a kind of rhythm—a dependable cycle that reinforces your credibility as a leader." I took his words to heart, realizing I'd been thinking about payroll just a little bit too narrowly.

Since implementing Gusto, I'd ensured that every paycheck arrived on time, without the delays that had once been our norm. The impact was noticeable across our job sites. Workers who had previously seemed anxious and frustrated were now more engaged and focused. There was definitely a new sense of professionalism—an acknowledgment that if you value your team, they'll value you back.

The transition hadn't been perfectly smooth. We'd encountered occasional technical issues, questions about handling bonuses, and the inevitable learning curve with any new system. But Gusto's support team had been responsive, and we'd worked through each challenge systematically.

One particular memory stands out: our first payday after fully implementing Gusto. I remember sitting in my office, refreshing my email until the confirmation arrived that payroll had processed successfully. I checked in with several team members, and their responses were overwhelmingly positive. "Money in my account—right on time," one texted. "Finally, no more wondering when we'll get paid," said another. This didn't feel like such a small victory, so I was happy.

In a follow-up call, Timothy reinforced this point. "You see how it changes everything when your team knows they can count on you," he said. "Timely payroll speaks for itself. It demonstrates respect, and that respect builds a motivated, stable workforce."

Our technology implementation hadn't stopped with Gusto. In parallel, we'd set up Bill.com for vendor and subcontractor payments, creating an equally impressive transformation in our external relationships. When suppliers and subcontractors began receiving prompt, consistent payments through Bill.com's automated system, our reputation as a reliable partner spread quickly. Projects that once felt like uphill battles started running more smoothly. Suppliers became more responsive, and subcontractors more eager to work with us. There was a tangible shift in how our business was perceived—internally through Gusto and externally through Bill.com.

With both systems in place, managing payments, taxes, and compliance became less daunting. Automated filings and detailed reports eliminated those evenings spent cross-checking numbers and worrying about missing deadlines. Instead, I could focus on strategic planning and business growth—and occasionally, for the first time in years, *actually relax*. The relief was truly profound, allowing me to step back and view the business with a fresh perspective.

The connection between reliable payment systems and overall business stability became increasingly clear. When employees received timely payments and tax compliance ran smoothly, the entire organization functioned better. Energy once wasted on friction and uncertainty now fueled genuine progress—visible not just in financial statements but in the atmosphere on job sites and the growth of client relationships.

Through this process, I learned that robust payment systems require regular monitoring and occasional adjustments. I kept a close eye on how things were running, aiming to catch potential issues early and ensure the systems continued meeting our evolving needs. I also made it a point to communicate clearly with the team about these systems during meetings, showing them that this technological investment reflected our commitment to valuing and respecting their contributions.

One particularly memorable Zoom call with Timothy encapsulated the process almost perfectly. "So, you're past the point of just paying salaries," he said. "You're investing in the very foundation of your business culture. Every time those automated payments go out, you're making a promise—that you care, that you're organized, and that you're committed to doing things right."

CHAPTER 17

IMPLEMENTING TECHNOLOGY WITHOUT LOSING YOUR MIND

There's a moment in every contractor's life when you stare at the technology tools you've chosen and wonder if they're truly going to be your salvation—or just another headache. I can actually remember the day I first faced that dilemma after Timothy had convinced me to adopt BuilderTrend, QuickBooks Online, Dext, and Bill.com. On one hand, I certainly craved the efficiency promised by these modern tools; on the other, I was absolutely terrified of the chaos that might follow if we didn't implement them properly.

One Friday morning, I logged into Zoom for my weekly check-in with Timothy. His friendly face appeared on screen. "Today," he began, "we're going to talk about implementing all these tools without feeling like you're losing your mind." The kind of blunt honesty that had become both my wake-up call and my north star.

I quickly felt a knot in my stomach. While I was excited about the tools we'd chosen, I'd seen promises of "the next big thing" come and go over the years. I'd even tried a few systems on my own before meeting Timothy—only to end up frustrated, overwhelmed by steep learning curves and disruptions to daily work. My team was already stretched thin by the demands of our projects, and the last thing I wanted was to add another layer of complexity. But Timothy's words were solid: proper implementation was the key to success with our new technology stack.

"Start small," Timothy advised during our call, leaning forward so his eyes locked with mine. "Don't try to implement everything at once. Pick one process that's causing you the most pain and focus on that tool first. Then, build from there." His advice was incredibly simple, but it seemed to strike a chord deep inside me. I realized that trying to overhaul everything at once would only lead to frustration. I'd be trying to reinvent the wheel while it was still rolling, and it would drive me mad.

I decided that the most pressing problem was our scheduling and project management. Our team was juggling multiple tasks, and communication often felt like a game of broken telephone. So even though we had purchased all four tools, I would focus on BuilderTrend first, since it addressed our most critical pain point. Instead of diving in headfirst, I took Timothy's advice: start small. I set up a pilot project in BuilderTrend, limited to one ongoing project that had been particularly chaotic. My goal was not to convert the whole business overnight but to see if this tool could bring some clarity to one troubled corner of our operations.

The first few days were rough. I spent hours setting up the system, inputting every task, deadline, and change order manually. I called in my team for a brief Zoom training session, expecting resistance and confusion. And sure enough, the reactions were mixed—some were skeptical, others overwhelmed. One of my long-time foremen, Joe, joked, "I'm not sure I signed up to become a digital cowboy!" His comment, though delivered with a laugh, revealed a truth I couldn't ignore: change was hard, especially when it disrupted habits honed over years on the job site.

Timothy reassured me during our follow-up call. "It's normal for there to be resistance at first," he said. "People don't change overnight. The key is to provide ongoing support and training, and to show them that BuilderTrend isn't there to replace them, but to make their jobs easier." He emphasized that patience was critical. "Start with one project, iron out the kinks, and then gradually expand its use to other projects. Only then should you move on to fully implementing the next tool."

Taking his words to heart, I arranged for a series of short, focused training sessions on BuilderTrend. Instead of a one-time, marathon session that would overwhelm everyone, I broke it into manageable chunks—one feature at a time. I recorded these sessions using Loom so that those who couldn't attend live could catch up later. I also created a simple Q&A document, gathering the most common issues and solutions that arose during our initial usage. Gradually, I began to see a shift. Joe started to nod along during meetings, asking practical questions rather than complaining. The team slowly began to appreciate the clarity of a shared digital schedule, where everyone knew exactly what was expected, and deadlines weren't lost in the shuffle of verbal communication.

Implementing BuilderTrend—like with any of the tools we'd chosen—wasn't a magic bullet, though. There were still moments of frustration—a mis-entered task here, a misunderstanding there. But instead of letting those hiccups derail the project, I started to view them as valuable feedback. Each error was an opportunity to refine our processes, to adjust the tool's settings, and to ensure that the system truly fit our workflow. I kept a notebook by my side (a habit I'd picked up from years of managing on paper), jotting down every issue and the corresponding solution. This iterative process, though slow, was important. It taught me that integrating technology was really all about gradual improvement, learning from mistakes, and building confidence in the new system.

Once BuilderTrend started to work smoothly on that pilot project, I felt comfortable expanding its use to other projects. The success of one project became a case study for the entire team. During our next all-hands Zoom meeting, I presented the results: fewer missed deadlines, clearer communication, and a marked improvement in tracking changes. The team's skepticism began to turn into optimism. I even started to receive unsolicited positive feedback from clients who noticed the enhanced organization on our projects.

With BuilderTrend gaining traction after about three months of focused implementation, I turned my attention to our next priority: QuickBooks Online. "Financial clarity is your next biggest need," Timothy advised. "Now that you've got project management under control with BuilderTrend, it's time to tackle the accounting side."

Following the same methodical approach, I worked closely with Maria, our bookkeeper, to optimize the integration between our existing QuickBooks Online system and BuilderTrend. We set aside dedicated time to ensure the two platforms were communicating effectively, created documentation specific to our data flow needs, and established a process for troubleshooting any synchronization issues. This integration phase became a particular focus, as the seamless flow of information between project management and accounting would be crucial for our overall efficiency. Fine-tuning this connection took about two months, during which we continued to refine our BuilderTrend processes simultaneously.

By month six of our technology implementation journey, with both BuilderTrend and QuickBooks Online functioning well, we were ready for the third piece: Dext for expense tracking. "Now that your core project and financial systems are stable, we can streamline the entire flow of expense data through your technology stack," Timothy explained during one of our check-ins. "With Dext, your receipts will be captured at the source, automatically flow into QuickBooks for accounting, and then populate BuilderTrend for accurate job cost reporting. It's all about creating that seamless data pipeline."

He walked me through the process flow: a receipt would be photographed and uploaded to Dext, which would extract the key information, push it to QuickBooks where it would be categorized and recorded, and finally appear in

BuilderTrend's job costing reports, allowing project managers to see real-time expense impacts on their budgets.

We initially focused on training just a few key team members who handled most of our receipts. As they became comfortable with the system and began to see the benefits of this automated data flow, they became advocates, helping to train others on the team. This phase took about six weeks to fully implement, but the result was worth it—a complete digital pipeline for expense data from initial capture through final job cost reporting.

Finally, in month eight, we implemented Bill.com for vendor payments, the last component of our technology stack. "This is the final piece that closes the loop in your financial workflow," Timothy said. "Now let me show you how the full cycle works." He walked me through the complete process: a vendor bill would first be entered into BuilderTrend where the project manager could review and approve it, then it would automatically flow into QuickBooks Online for accounting purposes, and finally be routed to Bill.com for payment processing.

"This is the beauty of a fully integrated system," Timothy explained as he demonstrated the workflow on his screen. "You enter data once in BuilderTrend, and it travels through your entire financial ecosystem without anyone having to manually re-enter it. The project manager approves it, your bookkeeper sees it in QuickBooks, and your vendors get paid through Bill.com—all from that single initial entry."

We set up clear approval workflows and ensured that everyone understood their role in this streamlined process. The entire implementation journey—from our first BuilderTrend pilot to having all four systems fully operational and integrated—took approximately ten months, but the efficiency gains were already proving worth every minute we'd invested.

Throughout this staged implementation, I learned that technology was just one piece of the puzzle. I had to remember that tools like BuilderTrend, QuickBooks Online, Dext, and Bill.com were only as good as the people using them. Timothy's advice was useful here: "Tools streamline operations, but they don't replace the need for good leadership and clear processes." So, alongside the new technology, I made sure to revisit our operating procedures. I worked with the team to update our workflows, ensuring that every step—from project initiation to final handover—was documented and aligned with our new digital tools. It wasn't enough to just implement the software; we had to create a culture where everyone embraced these changes and understood how they contributed to our overall success.

As we continued integrating these tools, I encountered technical glitches, unexpected downtime, and even moments when I questioned whether the investment was worth the effort. One particularly trying day, after a major update caused BuilderTrend to go offline for several hours, I felt that old panic creeping back in. Would this disrupt a critical project? Would we miss an important deadline? In that moment of uncertainty, I called Timothy. Over a half-hour Zoom call, he patiently walked me through troubleshooting steps, reassuring me that setbacks were just a part of the process. "Every tool has its growing pains," he said. "It's how you respond to those challenges that defines your success. Keep calm, document the issue, and work through it one step at a time."

As months passed, the benefits of our integrated technology stack started to manifest more clearly. BuilderTrend provided a central hub for project management, QuickBooks Online gave us accurate financial reporting, Dext simplified expense tracking, and Bill.com ensured timely vendor payments. The automated syncing between these systems meant that information flowed seamlessly across our business, reducing manual data entry and the potential for errors.

Our virtual meetings evolved as well. Instead of lengthy, drawn-out sessions where we'd try to cover every detail, we adopted a more agile approach—shorter, more frequent check-ins where we could address issues as they arose. The team began to share success stories and lessons learned from using our new tools, and gradually, the initial resistance faded away.

One afternoon, during a routine Zoom check-in with Timothy, he looked at me and said, "See, technology is your ally. It won't solve all your problems overnight, but it can give you the edge you need to stay ahead. The key is not to let it overwhelm you. Start small, learn continuously, and always keep your focus on what really matters: delivering quality work and building a sustainable business."

I nodded, reflecting on everything we'd achieved up to that point. We'd gone from a business relying on manual processes and disconnected systems to one where information flowed seamlessly between BuilderTrend, QuickBooks Online, Dext, and Bill.com. The transition hadn't been easy, but by taking a methodical, patient approach to implementation, we'd avoided the chaos that often comes with technological change.

"You know what I've learned?" I said to Timothy. "It's not just about having the right tools—it's about implementing them *the right way*. And that takes time, patience, and a willingness to learn from mistakes."

Timothy smiled. "Exactly. And now that you've got these tools working together smoothly, you're ready to take on bigger projects and grow your business with confidence."

He was right. Our technology stack had transformed from a source of stress to a competitive advantage. By implementing each tool thoughtfully and integrating them into a cohesive system, we'd created a foundation for sustainable growth. And perhaps most importantly, we'd done it without losing our minds in the process!

CHAPTER 18

WHEN TO BUY THE RIGHT TOOLS

One day, I almost made a costly mistake—buying a shiny new piece of equipment that, on paper, looked like it would revolutionize our workflow but ended up draining our cash flow faster than I could say "overextended." This week it was a Thursday afternoon that I was to get on a Zoom call with Timothy. I was feeling that familiar blend of excitement and apprehension that always came when it was time to talk money and investments. Timothy's face filled the screen. "You've got to learn to buy the right tools at the right time. Not every shiny gadget is worth the plunge."

I leaned back, rubbing my temples. "I know," I replied, "but sometimes it feels like every new tool promises to do wonders for us. How do I figure out which ones are really income-producing, and when it's safe to make the investment?" Timothy's response was as clear as it was blunt: "It's all about timing—understanding your cash flow, analyzing your workload, and projecting your growth. If you buy too soon, you overextend and risk everything. Wait too long, and you might miss the opportunity to really boost your profitability."

That conversation became a turning point for me. I realized that making tech investments wasn't just about having the latest software or gadget—it was about being strategic. Every dollar spent needed to serve a purpose, and every tool had to prove its worth by generating income or saving enough time to justify its cost.

Over the next few weeks, I dug deep into our financials. I started reviewing our cash flow reports with the meticulous care of someone who had learned the hard way that cash is king. I set aside time each week to project our growth, crunching numbers to determine when we'd have the extra funds available. I began to see patterns in our workloads—periods of relative calm interspersed with bursts of intense activity. These insights allowed me to pinpoint the perfect windows for making investments without jeopardizing our operations.

One evening, I was working late in the office, sifting through spreadsheets, when I had an epiphany. I remembered how my old habit of impulsively buying tools had nearly led to disaster—a memory of a pricey piece of equipment that had cost more in maintenance and downtime than it ever saved in productivity. I jotted down a rough checklist on a napkin:

Assess Current Workload: Are we consistently overloaded or just experiencing temporary peaks?

Review Cash Flow: What's our current financial cushion? How many months of overhead do we have?

Growth Projections: Is our business growing steadily enough to justify an expansion?

Income-Generating Potential: Will this tool immediately boost productivity, reduce errors, or cut down labor costs?

Integration and Training: How easily can the team adapt to this new tool, and what's the learning curve?

Armed with that checklist, I scheduled a follow-up Zoom call with Timothy. "I've been thinking about our conversation on tech investments," I said, the notebook filled with scribbled notes in front of me. "I've drafted a checklist to help me decide when it's the right time to buy new tools. What do you think?"

Timothy smiled. "That's exactly the kind of approach you need. Don't just buy because something's new or trendy—buy because it's the right fit for your business's current stage and your future growth." He walked me through his own process, explaining that he'd always looked for tools that were clearly income-producing. "When you see a tool that saves you an hour of work a day, that's money in your pocket. But if it's something that only looks good on paper, you might end up spending more time managing it than benefiting from it."

We spent the next hour dissecting various scenarios. Timothy showed me case studies—real-world examples of contractors who had made well-timed purchases that boosted their bottom line, and others who had jumped in too soon, only to find themselves strapped for cash. One story stuck with me: a contractor who had invested in an expensive piece of technology without thoroughly analyzing his cash flow, only to find that the tool didn't generate enough efficiency gains to cover its cost. The lesson was obvious: strategic timing isn't optional—it's critical.

I began to apply this thinking to our current needs. One area we had been struggling with was our heavy reliance on manual data entry for project management and accounting. We already had QuickBooks Online and Dext in place, but I wondered if there was a more integrated solution that could tie everything together. I started researching options, comparing features, costs, and user reviews. With our new checklist in hand, I carefully analyzed each tool, not just for its features, but for its potential to produce measurable results. I asked myself: Will this tool save me at least an hour a day? Will it reduce errors enough to prevent costly mistakes? Will it integrate seamlessly with our existing systems?

As I worked through this process, I began to see that our workload wasn't necessarily constant—it ebbed and flowed. During the busy season, every extra minute was precious, and a tool that saved even a small amount of time could be invaluable. In contrast, during slower periods, it might be wiser to hold off on a major investment until our cash flow was more robust. This nuanced understanding allowed me to plan for investments that wouldn't stretch our resources too thin.

As we expanded our use of new tools, I also made it a priority to train my team thoroughly. There was no point in buying the latest gadget if no one knew how to use it properly. I organized short, focused training sessions via Zoom, much like we had done with previous tools, ensuring that everyone—from the project managers to the field workers—understood the new system. I found that when people felt confident in using a tool, they not only used it more effectively, but they also became advocates for it. The culture shifted subtly but significantly. The team began to appreciate the new efficiencies, and I could see that the right investments, when timed correctly, could enhance productivity without overwhelming our operations.

Timothy often reminded me, "It's not about buying the most expensive or the flashiest tool—it's about buying the *right* tool that meets your current needs and supports your future growth." That insight guided every decision I made. I learned to resist the urge to chase every new trend and instead focus on what truly added value. I compared each potential purchase against our checklist: *Does it align with our workload? Can it be integrated without disrupting our current operations? Will it boost efficiency enough to justify its cost?* These questions became an integral part of my decision-making process.

The results of these carefully timed investments definitely started to show up on our balance sheets and in our day-to-day operations. We saw reduced turnaround times on projects, fewer errors in reporting, and a more streamlined workflow that allowed us to focus on growth rather than just merely *surviving*. Our team was less bogged down by administrative hassles, and the money saved on inefficiencies began to accumulate.

One evening, during another one of my routine Zoom calls with Timothy, I shared our latest progress. "Our project management tool has shaved off nearly 20% of our reporting time," I said, excitement in my voice. Timothy nodded, his expression satisfied. "That's the real power of strategic investments," he said. "When you buy the right tool at the right time, it transforms your entire operation."

CHAPTER 19

HOW TECHNOLOGY SAVES MONEY

After completing our ten-month journey of implementing our technology stack—QuickBooks Online first, then BuilderTrend, followed by Dext, and finally Bill.com —I could finally see the tangible benefits on our balance sheet. And it wasn't until I saw the tangible benefits on our balance sheet that I *truly* began to appreciate technology. One late afternoon, after reviewing our quarterly reports, I found myself thinking about a time when our projects were bogged down by manual processes and constant rework. The numbers were disheartening: wasted labor hours, missed deadlines, and error-ridden estimates that cost us more than they should have. That memory fueled a transformation that I now recognize as one of the smartest moves we ever made.

During a Zoom session one morning, Timothy shared a success story that still sticks with me. "I once worked with a contractor who was *drowning* in paperwork," he said. "He was using outdated methods for estimating jobs and tracking expenses. After switching to a modern accounting software and project management app, he slashed his overhead by nearly 15% in one year. *That* was technology doing what it's supposed to do: save money."

I leaned in, intrigued by the excitement in his voice. "15%?" I asked, almost in disbelief. Timothy nodded. "It's all in the details," he explained. "By automating repetitive tasks—like data entry, invoice processing, and expense tracking—you free up your team to focus on the work that really matters. And when you reduce human error, you not only save money, but you also build trust with your clients."

I began to see it more clearly. We'd been using QuickBooks Online for a while now, and every time I logged in, I noticed how much more organized our finances had become. Gone were the days of manually entering every expense into a clunky spreadsheet. With the integration of Dext, receipts were captured in real time and automatically fed into our accounting system. I recalled one instance where a misfiled receipt had once thrown off an entire month's budget—a mistake that cost us dearly in reconciliations and late fees. Now, every transaction was recorded precisely, and I could see immediately where every dollar was going.

The benefits weren't just about accounting, either. BuilderTrend, our project management tool, had turned what used to be a chaotic mess of emails, phone calls, and handwritten notes into a streamlined digital workflow. I remembered a particularly fraught project from a couple of years ago—one where miscommunications led to a cascade of change orders and a project that ran well over budget. Since integrating BuilderTrend, similar projects now run like a well-oiled machine! The app automated our scheduling, tracked our progress in real time, and even sent reminders to the team when deadlines were fast-approaching. The result was fewer delays, less wasted time, and a significant reduction in costly errors.

One success story that stands out in my mind is a mid-sized renovation project we undertook last year. The project had all the hallmarks of a potential disaster: a tight deadline, an incredibly complicated scope, and a history of miscommunication with subcontractors. In the past, I might have dreaded such a project, anticipating endless headaches and unforeseen costs. But this time, we were prepared. We had integrated our own suite of technologies that allowed us to manage every single aspect of the job digitally.

Before the project started, we used BuilderTrend to set up a detailed timeline, breaking the work into clear, manageable phases. Each phase was assigned specific tasks, and everyone—from the crew on the ground to the project manager—had access to the same up-to-date information. As the work progressed, our real-time tracking feature alerted us to a potential delay when one critical shipment was running late. Instead of scrambling last minute, I was able to make adjustments in advance, reassigning resources and communicating the change to everyone via the app. In the end, we finished the project two days ahead of schedule and under budget!

Timothy's practical advice about automation wasn't limited to project management and accounting. He also stressed how tools like Bill.com had revolutionized our payment process. I still remember the frustration of making late payments or forgetting to make a payment to one of our vendors, juggling multiple deadlines, and worrying about vendor relationships. Bill.com automated payment reminders, ensuring that we paid our suppliers on time (which really changed the game for us). This kind of consistency strengthened our credibility in the market. Vendors began to trust us more, and that trust translated into better deals and more reliable service.

During one Zoom call, Timothy asked, "Have you noticed how much smoother everything runs when you don't have to worry about the nitty-gritty of payment processing?" I recalled the night before, when I had to spend nearly three hours sorting through a backlog of vendor invoices manually. That night, I'd felt drained and defeated. Now, with Bill.com handling the process automatically, those hours were gone—replaced by a reliable, almost invisible system that worked in the background, freeing me to focus on growing the business.

There's a saying in construction: "Time is money." And with technology, every minute saved is a minute that can be reinvested in the business. Automating routine tasks not only cuts down on errors but also liberates valuable time. I began to see that when I wasn't bogged down by administrative hassles, I could devote more energy to what truly mattered—securing new projects, building relationships with clients, and developing innovative strategies for future growth.

I remember a moment when I was reviewing our monthly reports on QuickBooks Online. I noticed that the time we saved on data entry and reconciliation had directly translated into fewer overtime hours for our staff and, ultimately, lower labor costs. It wasn't a huge sum, but over time, those savings accumulated, contributing significantly to our bottom line. That was the real magic of technology: it was about creating efficiencies that had a measurable financial impact.

Even more, technology allowed us to catch problems *before* they spiraled. In the past, a small error in estimating could lead to a project spiraling out of control, costing us thousands of dollars. Now, with our integrated systems, we could detect these errors early and speak with the customer about changing the scope of work for the project. It was like having a built-in early warning system for our business—a way to identify potential pitfalls and address them before they became major issues.

I learned that technology saves money by reducing waste—waste of time, money, and resources. Every automated task meant less room for human error. Every integrated system meant that information was shared seamlessly across the board, reducing the likelihood of miscommunication.

One day, as I was closing out a particularly successful project, I found myself thinking about the incredible leap we'd taken. The transformation had become undeniable. The same business that once relied on chaotic spreadsheets and last-minute phone calls now operated with the precision of a well-tuned machine! The numbers on the balance sheet spoke for themselves—improved profit margins, reduced overhead, and a more predictable cash flow.

In a follow-up Zoom call with Timothy, I shared these results with pride (and humility). "I can't believe how much our numbers have improved," I said, scrolling through a series of charts that clearly illustrated our progress. Timothy's smile was subtle but genuine. "That's the key," he said. "You're getting the hang of it now."

By the end of our conversation, I felt a deep appreciation for the role technology had played in our turnaround. It wasn't always easy to adopt these new systems, and there were *plenty* of moments of frustration along the way. But as the benefits became tangible—through fewer errors, more efficient workflows, and ultimately, increased profitability—I realized that every cent spent on these tools was money well invested.

CHAPTER 20

WHY EVERY COMPANY'S NUMBERS LOOK DIFFERENT

I sat down for a Zoom call with Timothy one particular Tuesday morning and felt that familiar *sinking* feeling—like I was—for some reason—constantly comparing my business's numbers to those of other contractors, wondering why mine never quite measured up. Over the years, I'd assumed that if I simply tightened up our processes, our profit margins would naturally align with the so-called "industry standard." But as Timothy explained during that call, the truth is far more nuanced. Every company's numbers look different, and that's not only normal—it's actually expected.

Timothy started by breaking it down for me. "You see," he said, "there's no one-size-fits-all when it comes to financial profiles. Factors like geographic location, labor costs, project scopes, and even management styles can create vast differences in your numbers compared to another company that might seem similar on the surface." I sat up straight, absorbing his words.

He began with geographic location. "Think about it," Timothy said, "a contractor in a bustling urban area will have a very different cost structure than one operating in a smaller town." I recalled our own operations—situated on the outskirts of a growing mid-sized town, where labor was affordable and project scopes varied wildly. In contrast, a company in a major metropolitan center might face significantly higher overheads, from expensive labor to skyrocketing material costs. "Your numbers are a reflection of *where you operate*," he explained. "It's not that one company is doing something wrong—the circumstances are just *different*."

That perspective was eye-opening. I had often felt frustrated when comparing our profit margins and overhead to those of a larger competitor, thinking we were falling short. Now, I understood that our figures were inherently shaped by our environment. In our quieter, less expensive locale, a lower profit margin might actually be quite healthy, while in a high-cost market, even a slim margin could be a sign of efficiency.

Next, Timothy touched on labor costs. "Every company has to deal with the human element," he said. "But how you manage labor—and the costs associated with it—varies greatly. For instance, a company that invests in skilled, well-trained workers may have higher payroll expenses, but they also see fewer errors and less rework. Conversely, if you're hiring unskilled labor just to cut costs, those savings can quickly evaporate when mistakes add up." I remembered our own early missteps—hiring shortcuts that resulted in poor workmanship and constant rework. It was a painful lesson in how trying to save money upfront could lead to greater expenses down the line. Timothy's words made it clear that labor costs, and the way they're managed, are a critical part of your financial profile—and one that can't be judged in isolation.

Then came project scopes. "Not every project is created equal," Timothy said. "Some jobs are small and straightforward, while others are massive, complex undertakings that require detailed planning and higher upfront investment. Naturally, the financial dynamics of these projects will look very different." I thought back to a couple of years ago when we'd taken on a renovation project that spiraled out of control—each change order, each unexpected expense, had pushed our numbers right into the red. On the other hand, there were projects where we'd delivered *exactly* on target, with a neat alignment between our estimates and actual costs. The variability in project scope meant that comparing numbers across different types of jobs wasn't just unfair—it was actually very misleading.

Finally, Timothy talked about management styles. "This is something people often overlook," he said. "How you run your business—how you communicate, how you plan, how you execute—has a huge impact on your financial results." I had always prided myself on being hands-on, diving into every project and trying to micromanage every detail. But as Timothy pointed out many times before, that approach, while it might work for some, often leads to inefficiencies and burnout. A more strategic, delegative style can streamline operations, reduce errors, and ultimately improve profitability.

During that Zoom call, I found myself scribbling down notes furiously, trying to capture every single insight. He shared stories of other contractors who had faced similar frustrations. One contractor had tried to mimic the financial profile of a larger company, only to find that his overheads were completely different because of his local market and his unique approach to labor management. Another had discovered that his project estimates were always off because he was comparing apples to oranges—basing his numbers on projects that weren't even similar in scope to his own. "The key," Timothy stressed, "is to analyze your business on its own terms. Look at your history, understand your environment, and tailor your strategies accordingly."

That was really a turning point for me. I began to see (and understand) that comparing our numbers to those of other companies was really just a futile exercise. Each business was its own ecosystem, shaped by a unique set of factors that made direct comparisons nearly meaningless. Instead of feeling inadequate or frustrated, I started to embrace the idea that our numbers were simply *our* numbers—a reflection of our particular circumstances, our choices, and our approach.

Over the following weeks, I dove into our financial data with a fresh perspective. I reviewed our profit margins, labor costs, overheads, and cash flow, but this time, *I did it on my own terms*. I compared our figures with our own historical data, looking for trends and patterns that could help me understand where we had improved and where we still had work to do. I was trying to understand our story.

For instance, I noticed that our profit margins had been steadily improving over the past year, even if they weren't as high as those of a competitor in a high-cost urban center. I learned to appreciate that improvement in context—it wasn't about being the best in the world, but about being better than we had been *yesterday*. Similarly, when I looked at our direct labor efficiency ratios, I saw that while there were occasional dips, the overall trend was positive. Each dip had a story behind it—sometimes a particularly challenging project, sometimes a temporary shortage of skilled workers—and by understanding those stories, I could adjust our strategies to prevent future issues.

I also took a hard look at our overhead costs. There was a tendency, I realized, to lump certain expenses together and assume that a high overhead was always a sign of inefficiency. But when I broke down our costs by category, I saw that some of what I'd always considered overhead was actually an investment in quality and reliability—expenses that, while high, were necessary to support our operations in our specific market. This level of detailed analysis allowed me to set realistic expectations for our business, tailored not to some generic ideal but to our actual performance and potential.

Throughout this process, I became more confident in my ability to use KPIs as a reliable guide for navigating our business. Instead of being overwhelmed by the sheer volume of numbers, I learned to focus on the ones that truly mattered for our specific circumstances. I started to see that the "truth" in the numbers was a story that each business tells about itself, influenced by a multitude of factors that only it can fully understand.

Timothy's parting words during that Zoom call still stick with me to this very day: "Don't compare your chapter one to someone else's chapter ten. Your numbers tell your story, and it's up to you to write the next chapter." That simple, honest reminder freed me from the trap of constant comparison. I began to appreciate our financial profile as something uniquely ours—a tool to guide our decisions, celebrate our improvements, and learn from our setbacks.

In the months that followed, I set up regular reviews of our key performance indicators, using them not as a measure of how we stacked up against others, but as a roadmap for our own growth as a company. I established benchmarks based on our history, and I set realistic, incremental goals. Each month, I would sit down with the data, celebrate our tiny victories—a slight uptick in profit margins here, a reduction in labor costs there—and adjust our strategies wherever they needed to be adjusted.

I also shared these insights with my team during our weekly Zoom meetings. Instead of comparing ourselves to the big players in the industry, we focused on *our own* progress. We talked about how every project, every effort to reduce waste, and every small improvement in efficiency was a real step forward for us. It became about outdoing *ourselves*. The team began to see that our success was determined by our own dedication to continually improve, and our willingness to adapt to our very unique circumstances.

CHAPTER 21

BRIDGING THE GAP BETWEEN FIELD AND BACK OFFICE

By this point, we had already built out a solid technology stack—BuilderTrend, QuickBooks, Dext, Gusto, and B ill.com. The problem wasn't the software. The problem was getting the field and the back office to actually use it the right way—consistently. That disconnect was still costing us time, money, and, most importantly, trust.

I still remember those early implementation days clearly. At first, we faced a recurring challenge: missing or incomplete data inBuilderTrend. I'd start each morning with frantic calls from the back office—reports were incomplete, hours weren't being logged consistently, and critical details were lost in translation. In the field, my crew was understandably focused on safety and deadlines; updating the app often fell to the bottom of their priority list. Meanwhile, our back office team struggled to piece together a puzzle with missing pieces. Even with our impressive new tech stack, this initial disconnect created inefficiencies that slowed our progress.

But that was then. Looking back at those growing pains helps me appreciate how far we've come. The same technology that once felt like another burden has now become the backbone of our seamless operation. The key wasn't just having the right tools—it was developing the right habits and culture around using them.

One day, as I was reviewing yet another incomplete report on a particularly messy project, I logged into my Zoom call with Timothy. His face, as always, was a blend of practicality and a hint of humor, as if he knew exactly where I was headed.

"You know," he said, leaning forward, "the field and the back office aren't separate worlds—they're really more like two sides of the same coin. If you don't learn how to bridge that gap, you're basically running two different businesses."

I nodded. Timothy's words cut through my frustration like a clear, cold breeze.

He continued, "You already have the right tools with BuilderTrend,QuickBooks, Dext, Gusto, and Bill.com. The problem isn't the technology—it's how you're using it. The data needs to flow seamlessly from the field to the back office every single day. This is a team effort, not just an individual responsibility."

Timothy was right. We had invested in the perfect construction tech stack, but we weren't maximizing its potential.

The disconnect wasn't due to a lack of tools; it was due to inconsistent processes and unclear expectations.

Timothy nodded approvingly as we reviewed our field team's growing mastery of the system. "What I love about what you're doing is the constant refinement," he said. "Your crew already understands the basics—clocking in and out, documenting materials, capturing site photos—but now they're seeing how their consistent inputs create this beautiful data ecosystem that benefits everyone. It's like watching a team that's learned to play the notes perfectly now start to make actual music together." He smiled as we scrolled through the dashboard. "This isn't about fixing problems anymore—it's about taking something that works and making it exceptional."

I decided it was time to refocus on making our existing technology work for us. The solution wasn't adopting new software—we already had BuilderTrend for that—but rather creating a culture where data entry was seen as an essential part of the job, not an afterthought.

I organized a series of short, practical training refreshers, held virtually over Zoom. We walked through BuilderTrend step by step, focusing specifically on the daily tasks that needed to be completed without fail: time tracking, progress updates, material usage, and photo documentation. I made sure to include plenty of real-world examples showing how incomplete data had caused problems in our workflow.

"Think of it this way," I told my team during one session. "When you don't log your hours or update job progress in BuilderTrend, it's like trying to build a house without measurements. The back office can't do their job if they don't have accurate information from the field."

Slowly, things began to change. My team started to take ownership of their role in the data flow. Instead of just going through the motions, they started seeing how their updates directly impacted job scheduling, payroll, and budgets. There were, of course, still occasional lapses, a few miscommunications, and plenty of questions. But with every hiccup, we refined our processes, adjusted our training, and learned just a little more about how to make the system work for us.

One particular day stands out when I think about it now. It was the first time I checked BuilderTrend's dashboard after a full week of consistent usage by everyone. There, in clear, digital lines and graphs, was the complete picture of our daily operations: crew hours, task completions, even visual documentation of progress through photos. I could see that everything was running smoother than it had in years. No more frantic calls asking, "Where's the data?" No more guessing games with incomplete information.It was all there, updated in real time, and it made decision-making a whole lot less stressful.

Timothy was thrilled during one of our subsequent Zoom calls."That's the power of integration," he said, smiling. "When your field and your back office speak the same language through BuilderTrend, everything flows beautifully from there to QuickBooks and the rest of your systems. It cuts down on errors, reduces chaos, and builds trust—not just between you and your team, but among the team itself."

I realized that every miscommunication, every missing piece of data, had been a barrier between the people on the job site and the people in the back office. Bridging that gap created a cohesive, united operation where every person knew their role and could see how their work contributed to the bigger picture.

I started to see changes beyond just the numbers. The team began to work with a new kind of energy. Instead of seeing BuilderTrend updates as a chore, they started to appreciate the immediate feedback the system provided. When a foreman entered time correctly, the back office had everything needed for smooth payroll processing in Gusto. When a project update was posted with photos, it created a permanent record of achievement that everyone could see and appreciate. The flow of information transformed into a flow of trust between all of my employees.

My back office no longer operated in isolation, hidden behind walls of emails and phone calls; it became an active, dynamic part of the day-to-day work on the site. With BuilderTrend connecting everyone, my project managers could spend less time chasing down information and more time on-site, where they could actually see progress.

Over time, the gap between the field and the back office narrowed to almost nothing. Standardized processes replaced the inconsistent methods. Clear expectations were set, and everyone knew exactly what was required of them, every single day. And with consistent communication—thanks to regular Zoom meetings, real-time BuilderTrend updates, and Timothy's guidance—the entire team began to function as one cohesive unit, rather than two separate entities.

There were still challenges, of course—there always will be! Maintaining discipline with daily data entry is never going to happen without a little bit of friction. There were days when someone would forget to clock out of a job, or connectivity issues on remote sites would delay photo uploads. But instead of letting those setbacks spiral into crises, I began to see them as opportunities to dive in and refine our approach.

We'd hold quick troubleshooting sessions over Zoom, where team members would share their experiences, and we'd work together to find solutions. Each small problem solved was a step toward a more reliable workflow, and with every improvement, the gap grew even smaller.

One day, after a particularly smooth week, I received an email from one of our senior project managers. "I can't believe how much easier it is now that everyone is actually using BuilderTrend properly," he wrote. "I spend less time chasing down information and more time focusing on what matters. It's like the old barriers between the field and the back office have just melted away. Thank you!"

Reading that email, I felt relief. Heck, I felt proud!

We had managed to bridge a gap that had long been a source of frustration and inefficiency, and in doing so, we had built a foundation for a more agile and responsive business. The key wasn't finding new technology—it was making the most of what we already had.

And the impact was bigger than just fewer headaches. With accurate data flowing from the field, we could finally trust our numbers. Labor hours, material costs, job progress—all of it was now crystal clear. No more guessing when a job was running over budget. No more surprises in payroll. For the first time, our financial reports reflected reality, not just best guesses.

That changed everything. And as I'd soon realize, understanding those numbers was the key to running a profitable business—not just a busy one.

Chapter 22

Systems That Connect the Field to the Office

After nearly a year of methodically rolling out our tech stack, we were finally seeing how it all came together to bridge the gap between the field and the back office. We started with QuickBooks Online, Dext, and Gusto—usually implemented together over the first one to three months—before introducing BuilderTrend in the second month, which would take up to nine months for full adoption. By month eight, we added Bill.com to the mix, rounding out a system designed to streamline communication, improve accountability, and bring clarity to every part of the business.

One afternoon, I was on a Zoom call with Timothy, tea in hand per usual, feeling that familiar blend of excitement and trepidation that always came with evaluating our progress. This time, Timothy wasn't talking about new tools or financial strategies; he was giving me his take on how well we were connecting the dots between our job sites and our back office using our existing technology stack.

"Communication is the heartbeat of any business," Timothy said, leaning into the camera with a serious look. "Now that you've implemented BuilderTrend, QuickBooks, Dext, Bill.com, and Gusto, let's make sure you're maximizing how these systems work together. When your field and back office are in sync through these tools, you eliminate room for errors, delays, and missed opportunities."

I nodded, recalling the countless mornings before we'd implemented these systems, when I'd get frantic messages about missing reports or unrecorded hours. "I feel like we're in a good spot now, but please, let's make sure I've got the workflow right," I said, ready to confirm our process.

Timothy smiled. "Let's walk through the entire workflow to make sure everything is connected properly. BuilderTrend is your field hub, but it's also the command center for you and your project coordinator who are constantly moving between jobs and the back office. QuickBooks is primarily your back office accounting engine. Dext handles receipt capture in the field, and Bill.com manages your payment process from the back office."

Over the next hour, Timothy helped me visualize the perfect workflow between these systems:

"Your project coordinator uploads bills from suppliers and subcontractors directly to BuilderTrend," he explained. "Then, your project manager – who's out in the field – can review and approve those bills right from the app if supplies were delivered as expected or if the subcontractor completed their work satisfactorily."

I could see how this eliminated the old back-and-forth where field supervisors would have to call the back office to confirm deliveries or work completion. Now it was all documented in real-time within BuilderTrend.

"Meanwhile," Timothy continued, "your field team uploads photos of job progress directly to BuilderTrend. This allows you as the owner to review progress from anywhere, and you can even grant clients access to see the progression of their projects."

This feature had already proven incredibly valuable. Just last week, a client had questions about a particular phase of their project, and instead of scheduling a site visit, I was able to show them the daily progress photos right from my tablet.

"Once the project manager approves bills in BuilderTrend and marks them ready for payment, your accounting team can seamlessly pay them using Bill.com," Timothy explained. "They can have checks mailed to vendors or sent via direct deposit. No more manual check writing or bank visits."

The payment workflow had dramatically reduced our processing time. What used to take hours of coordination between field approvals and back office payments now happened with just a few clicks.

Timothy then addressed another crucial connection: "When your field team captures receipts with Dext – whether it's for materials, fuel, or other expenses – your accounting team can publish them directly to QuickBooks, which automatically updates the job cost budget report in BuilderTrend."

This was one of the most significant improvements we'd made. Before implementing these systems, we'd often discover budget overruns only after a project was completed. Now, our project managers could see in real-time if a project was running over or under budget.

"And don't forget," Timothy added, "when your field team clocks in and out of jobs using BuilderTrend, their hours and costs get automatically booked to the job costing budget report. This gives your project managers immediate visibility into labor costs, and that time can be exported directly to Gusto for payroll processing."

Over the next few weeks, I observed our team working with this connected system. The technology we'd implemented – BuilderTrend, QuickBooks, Dext, Bill.com, and Gusto – had created a seamless flow of information between the field and back office that I'd only dreamed of before.

I watched as our foreman, Mike, who had been skeptical at first, embraced BuilderTrend fully. When a sudden equipment issue delayed part of a job, he simply used the app to report the problem and upload photos. Instantly, I received a notification, and so did our project coordinator in the back office. Within minutes, we had arranged for a replacement to be delivered, all without a single phone call.

During a midday break, I checked a job in BuilderTrend. There it was – a neatly organized report showing every hour logged, every expense recorded, and every bill approved. The integration with QuickBooks meant our financial picture was always up-to-date. "I'll never get tired of this," I said to myself, letting out a sigh of relief.

No longer was I left piecing together fragments of information from scattered sources. Everything was right there, updated as it happened, flowing seamlessly between BuilderTrend in the field and QuickBooks in the back office, with Dext capturing receipts, Bill.com handling payments, and Gusto processing payroll. That integrated flow of information was like a breath of fresh air, cutting through the old chaos.

Of course, the transition hadn't been without challenges. Integrating these systems into our daily workflow required more than just installing apps; it demanded a cultural shift. Some team members who had grown accustomed to the old ways were initially resistant to change. To overcome this, I organized practical training sessions over Zoom, walking through each function with the crew. I remember one session where I demonstrated the complete workflow: how to log hours in BuilderTrend, how those hours would flow to the budget report and eventually to Gusto for payroll; how to upload receipts through Dext and see them appear in QuickBooks and BuilderTrend; how to approve bills in BuilderTrend and watch them move to Bill.com for payment.

A young crew member hesitantly asked, "What if I lose internet connection on site? How do I handle that?" I explained that BuilderTrend had offline capabilities – he could still record information, and it would sync automatically once connectivity was restored. His relieved smile said it all.

Timothy's voice would often echo in my mind during these training sessions. "The key is consistency," he'd remind me. "Don't let a few hiccups derail the entire process. Every system takes time to settle in, but if you stick with it, you'll see the benefits."

As weeks turned into months, the integration of BuilderTrend, QuickBooks, Dext, Bill.com, and Gusto transformed our operations. The complete workflow we'd established created a single digital ecosystem where information flowed automatically between systems:

1. Project coordinators would upload supplier bills to BuilderTrend
2. Project managers would approve these bills from the field
3. Approved bills would flow to QuickBooks for accounting
4. Final payment would be processed through Bill.com
5. Field expenses captured in Dext would feed into QuickBooks and update BuilderTrend reports
6. Time tracked in BuilderTrend would streamline payroll in Gusto

This integration eliminated the information gaps that had once plagued us. When one project's material costs began exceeding estimates, I spotted it immediately in BuilderTrend's real-time reports and could address it before it became a significant problem.

"It's like we've finally stopped playing telephone," one of my senior project managers remarked during a team meeting. "Every piece of information flows exactly where it needs to go, and we're all working with the same data."

That comment captured it perfectly. Our tech stack had become the common language unifying field and back office, building trust throughout the organization. While we occasionally faced technical hiccups with the integration, each challenge we solved strengthened our system and our team's ability to use it effectively.

By the time I looked back at those early, tumultuous days, the transformation was nothing short of remarkable. The chaos of missing reports, miscommunication, and endless follow-up calls was replaced by a steady flow of accurate data between BuilderTrend, QuickBooks, Dext, Bill.com , and Gusto.

Today, as I sit at my desk and glance at the BuilderTrend dashboard that displays real-time updates from every project – updates that seamlessly connect to our accounting in QuickBooks, our receipt management in Dext, our payment processing in Bill.com, and our payroll in Gusto – I feel an incredible sense of accomplishment.

The systems we've put in place have become the connective tissue that binds our entire operation together. They allow us to make informed decisions quickly, respond to issues before they escalate, and create a work environment where everyone is both aligned and empowered.

Timothy's guidance was crucial throughout this journey. His insistence on maximizing the integration between our existing tools – BuilderTrend, QuickBooks, Dext, Bill.com, and Gusto – rather than constantly seeking new solutions kept me focused during the entire transition.

"You don't need more tools," he often reminded me. "You need to master the ones you have and ensure they're working together seamlessly." Those words proved to be some of the most valuable advice I'd received, setting us on a path to a more efficient, collaborative, and successful construction business.

CHAPTER 23

SCALING WITHOUT SINKING

I remember the moment everything changed. It wasn't when our systems were finally in place, or when our team was fully staffed—it was the Friday afternoon I found myself on the golf course with a potential client instead of on a job site checking measurements. As we discussed their vision for a new commercial property over the back nine, I realized I hadn't worried about a single operational detail all day! Our projects were running smoothly without my constant oversight, and for the first time, I was free to focus on what truly mattered: *growing* the business.

As you know, this did *not* happen overnight. Just months earlier, I had been drowning in details, micromanaging every aspect of our operations. During one particularly hectic Zoom call with Timothy, I admitted that a critical deadline was in jeopardy precisely because I'd been too busy checking everyone's work instead of letting my capable team do their jobs.

"You're drowning in details," he said. "When you try to do everything yourself, you're not just overworked—you're becoming the bottleneck that slows the whole operation down."

Those words—as always—hit me like a brick. I'd always prided myself on being hands-on, believing that if I was involved in every decision, I could steer the ship safely through turbulent waters. But as Timothy continued, I realized my constant interference was dragging down the potential of my growing team. *There was no external problem*—I was the one getting in the way!

"Scaling isn't about working harder," he added. "It's about working smarter. And that means learning to delegate—trusting the people you've carefully selected to do their jobs without your constant oversight. Your real role should be business development—finding new opportunities, building relationships, and planning strategic growth."

That conversation sparked a fundamental shift in my approach. I began analyzing our operations critically, identifying areas where I'd been holding on too tightly. I started delegating tasks that didn't require my direct intervention, trusting my team members to handle day-to-day details. During one pivotal Zoom session with my core crew, I said, "I've realized that if I continue trying to control every detail, I'm going to sink this business before it can really take off. From now on, I need you to own your roles fully. I'm not here to micromanage; I'm here to guide and support you."

The team seemed to breathe a collective sigh of relief—finally, I was giving them room to shine.

As I stepped back from daily operations, something remarkable happened: I began seeing opportunities everywhere. With BuilderTrend, QuickBooks, Dext, Bill.com, and Gusto working together seamlessly, our team had the tools they needed to operate with minimal oversight. Our project managers handled scheduling and client communications with confidence. Our site superintendents maintained quality control and kept crews on task. Our office staff processed invoices, managed payroll, and kept our financials in perfect order.

For the first time, I had mental space to think about the future. I started attending industry networking events, joining the local builders' association, and even scheduling regular golf outings with potential clients—something I'd never had time for before. These relationships began bearing fruit almost immediately, bringing in larger, more profitable projects than we'd ever handled.

During a check-in with Timothy, I shared how liberating it felt to focus on business development. "I closed two major contracts last week on the golf course," I told him, unable to hide my excitement. "Meanwhile, our team completed three projects on time and under budget without me visiting the sites more than once a week."

Timothy smiled. "This is exactly what I've been waiting for. You've finally stepped into your true role as a business owner. You're not just running a company anymore—you're *growing* it."

With our systems running smoothly and our team operating at peak efficiency, I found myself thinking *even bigger*. I began researching smaller construction companies that might make good acquisition targets, analyzing how their specialties could complement our existing services. I started exploring small real estate development opportunities—something I'd always dreamed about but never had bandwidth to pursue.

One particularly ambitious idea took root: developing a small mixed-use property on a lot I'd had my eye on for years. With our construction capabilities and newfound organizational strength, we could handle the project ourselves while continuing our client work. It would be our first step toward building a portfolio of income-producing properties alongside our construction business.

When I mentioned this to Timothy, he nodded approvingly. "Now you're thinking like a true entrepreneur. When your company runs itself, your only limitation is your imagination."

By year's end, we had not only exceeded our revenue targets but expanded into two new service areas. I was spending three days a week on business development, meeting potential clients, exploring acquisition opportunities, and planning our first development project. The other two days, I conducted strategic planning sessions with our leadership team, focusing on long-term growth rather than day-to-day operations.

The financial rewards were substantial, but the personal transformation was even more valuable. For the first time since starting the business, I took a two-week vacation with my family—*completely disconnected from work*—and returned to find everything running perfectly. Our digital dashboards showed all projects on track, with profitability metrics exceeding targets across the board.

In our final meeting of the year, Timothy asked me a simple question: "What's next?"

I smiled, feeling a sense of possibility I hadn't experienced in years. "We're looking at acquiring a specialized electrical contractor that would expand our service offerings. I'm in talks with an investor group about a joint venture on a larger development project. And we're evaluating whether to open a second office in the neighboring county."

Timothy nodded. "That's what happens when you build a business that doesn't depend on you for every decision. You get to dream again."

And he was right. After years of struggling to stay afloat, of micromanaging every detail and exhausting myself in the process, I'd finally built a construction company that could thrive without my constant attention. I'd assembled the right team, implemented the right systems, and learned to let go—creating space for growth I never thought possible.

CHAPTER 24

MISTAKES I WON'T MAKE AGAIN

If you're reading this, you're likely a construction business owner looking for guidance. Let me share something valuable with you—the costly mistakes I've made so you don't have to repeat them. Every successful construction company stands on the foundation of lessons learned the hard way, and mine is no exception. The difference between those who thrive and those who merely survive comes down to this: *are you willing to learn from your mistakes and transform them into something more?*

I've built my success on failures that once threatened to destroy everything I'd worked for. Overestimated growth, neglected financial oversight, poor hiring decisions, and a stubborn refusal to ask for help—these weren't just minor setbacks. They were fundamental flaws in my business approach that nearly cost me everything.

For years, I convinced myself that sheer determination would overcome any obstacle. I thought if I just worked hard enough, pushed every project over the finish line, everything would magically fall into place. But I was building on a foundation riddled with cracks. The breaking point came during what should have been a milestone project, which instead collapsed under missed deadlines and mounting costs. I had severely overestimated our capacity, taken on more than we could handle, and when the inevitable problems began, the pressure became unbearable.

Timothy's guidance helped me see these failures as the warning signs they truly were. "You've been so busy chasing growth," he told me during one of our early Zoom sessions, "that you forgot to check the foundation. That's where it all starts! You know you can't build a skyscraper on a shaky base."

One of my most costly mistakes was neglecting financial oversight. I thought I could manage everything by gut instinct, ignoring the numbers until they *screamed* for attention—profit margins dipping unexpectedly, cash flow turning erratic, expenses ballooning out of control. I still remember those anxiety-filled nights spent reconciling accounts, each miscalculation bringing me one step closer to disaster.

"If you can't account for every cent, you're just gambling with your future," Timothy said during a late-night Zoom call that changed my perspective forever. He showed me how to build robust accounting systems using tools like QuickBooks Online and Dext, ensuring no expense went untracked. What I once viewed as burdensome financial discipline became the very backbone of our sustainable growth.

Another critical mistake was my approach to hiring. I prioritized speed over quality, filling positions quickly and postponing proper training. This created a revolving door of unqualified workers, each adding to the inefficiencies plaguing our projects. I recall hiring a foreman solely because he offered the lowest rate, only to watch his inexperience transform a straightforward job into a logistical nightmare.

"The right people will save you time, money, and your reputation," Timothy emphasized. "It's better to hire slowly and fire fast than to settle for mediocrity." Implementing rigorous hiring processes—including the KOLBE assessment and Strength Assessment by Ministry Insights—transformed our team. Patience in hiring yielded a competent, motivated crew that could handle challenges without constant supervision.

Perhaps my most persistent mistake was refusing to delegate. I micromanaged every detail, convinced my hands-on approach was essential to success. This created a bottleneck that slowed progress and left me exhausted. I believed if I wasn't involved in every decision, the business would crumble. Timothy helped me see the truth: by clinging to control, I was stunting both my team's growth and the business's potential.

"Your value as a leader is never going to be in doing every single thing yourself," Timothy explained during one particularly transformative conversation. "It's in creating an environment where your team can take ownership, where everyone knows their role and operates independently. When you delegate effectively, you free up your time to focus on strategic growth."

This forced me to confront an uncomfortable truth: my reluctance to delegate stemmed from *insecurity*. Gradually, I learned to trust my team, setting clear expectations and conducting regular check-ins without micromanaging. The results were transformative—team members rose to the challenge, operations ran more smoothly, and I regained the time and energy to focus on growing the business.

Over time, these hard lessons settled into wisdom. I documented them not as regrets but as actionable guidelines to prevent future missteps. This became a manual of sorts—filled with protocols for financial oversight, hiring procedures, and delegation strategies. Each entry represented hard-won knowledge that's now embedded in how we operate.

"Learning from your mistakes is the first step to building something that can truly last," Timothy told me. "Now, take those lessons and use them as building blocks. Let them guide you, but don't let them hold you back."

I've come to see my failures not as burdens but as invaluable teachers that shaped me into a better leader. I share these insights with my team regularly, fostering a culture where mistakes are opportunities to learn rather than reasons for blame. In our weekly meetings, we focus not on failures themselves but on lessons learned and strategies for improvement.

There will always be moments when old fears resurface—the worry that I might slip back into bad habits or that one miscalculation could undermine our progress. But with each passing day, I grow more confident in the blueprint we've created. I know exactly which mistakes I'll *never* repeat:

overestimating growth without financial backing, hiring impulsively, or micromanaging every detail.

Looking back on those turbulent early days, I recognize them as necessary trials on my path to success. Though painful, they forced me to reevaluate everything about my business approach, transforming it from frantic desperation to deliberate, strategic planning.

"Mistakes," as Timothy wisely put it, "are not the end of the road; they're the beginning of something new, something fresh. They're what tells you where you've been, so you know exactly where you need to go."

The true measure of a business isn't how many mistakes you've made but what you've learned from them. I've rebuilt processes, restructured my team, and redefined leadership—all because I faced my past head-on. While I can't erase those mistakes, I ensure they'll never define my future.

Today, I stand confident in the blueprint created from those hard lessons. I'm no longer the person who believed working nonstop and handling everything personally was the key to success. I've learned to delegate, to trust, and to value every lesson failure has taught me.

So if you're struggling with your construction business, know this: your mistakes aren't the end of your story—they're the beginning of a better one. Embrace them, learn from them, and transform them into the foundation of your future success. The path forward isn't about avoiding every mistake; *it's about ensuring you never make the same one twice.*

Chapter 25

Blueprints for the Future

Among the many mornings, I remember one in particular where I felt the kind of peace I always hear people talking about in movies. It was a quiet morning, the kind when the world seems to pause just for a moment. I sat in my office thinking about the long, tumultuous journey that had brought me to this very moment. Every single decision, every single mistake, every single Zoom call with Timothy had led me here, and now I could see clearly the blueprint for the future.

Looking back, it's hard not to feel a deep sense of gratitude for Timothy, and for how far we've come. I'll never forget when I first started this second attempt at building a construction business. I had made so many mistakes—overestimating growth, neglecting my finances, hiring the wrong people, and trying to do everything myself—that I often wondered if I was doomed to repeat history. But Timothy's professionalism and expertise has helped me turn those failures into a real roadmap for success.

Now, as I survey our operations on a daily basis, I can clearly see a business that's built on solid pillars: a clear vision, a strong, well-trained team, effective technology that streamlines our every move, and sustainable operations that ensure we're ready for whatever comes next.

My vision for the business is now crystal clear. No longer am I chasing every project that comes my way or trying to mimic someone else's success. No, instead, I've carved out a trajectory that reflects our unique strengths, our local market, and our dedication to quality and integrity. I've learned to measure our success by tracking our own progress—understanding the need to celebrate every improvement in efficiency, every project delivered on time, and every client who trusted us with their dream.

Our team, once a patchwork of misfits and hastily hired labor, has turned into a cohesive, motivated unit. We've learned to trust each other's expertise, and to support one another in ways I really never thought possible. The culture here is one that's *always* improving. I can see that change every day in the way that we communicate, both on the job site and in our virtual meetings.

Technology, too, cannot be overstated! Tools like BuilderTrend, QuickBooks Online, Dext, and Bill.com have become the very backbone of our operations. They've quite literally turned chaos into clarity, automating repetitive tasks, reducing errors, and providing real-time insights that guide our decisions. To the early days of implementing these systems—nervous training sessions, initial resistance from some crew members, and the inevitable hiccups along the way. With persistence, we integrated these tools into our workflow, and the payoff was absolutely undeniable: increased efficiency, better communication, and a steady stream of reliable data that helped us avoid costly mistakes. Today, our digital dashboard is like a pulse check on the business, keeping us informed and ready to act!

Sustainable operations have become a must. We've overhauled our processes, from hiring and training to financial management and project execution. Every decision is made with an eye on longevity. I'm proud to say that I've learned to balance short-term needs with long-term goals, ensuring that every tool, every process, and every hire adds value and strengthens our foundation.

I have to admit, there were many moments along the way when the pressure felt a little too unbearable. Late nights filled with data analysis, stressful phone calls with vendors, and the ever-present fear of repeating past mistakes kept me awake more often than I'd like to remember. But with each challenge, I grew a little stronger, a little more confident in my ability to steer the ship. And now, looking back on those hard-won lessons, I realize that it wasn't all for nothing. I'm no longer the owner who does everything himself—no more DIY. I've become a leader who aims to inspire and empower, who trusts in the strength of his team and the power of a clear, thoughtful strategy.

"You're not defined by your failures," Timothy once told me during one of our many Zoom calls, "but by what you do after them." I live by those words, and so do my team members. I've quite literally turned Timothy's lessons into requirements for my team. Any new member we bring aboard learns what Timothy has taught me.

And now, as I plan for the future, I'm filled with only optimism and purpose. I truly feel that I have a clear blueprint that outlines every aspect of our strategy moving forward. I'm excited to share this blueprint with you, not just as a personal achievement, but as a roadmap for other construction business owners who are struggling with the same challenges I once faced. I know you're out there!

In fact, I'm thrilled to announce, on Timothy's behalf, that he'll soon be launching an online course designed specifically for contractors who want practical strategies to build better businesses. This course will encapsulate everything I've learned—from financial management and team building to technology integration and sustainable growth. It's a chance for Timothy to pass on the lessons that transformed my business, to help others avoid the pitfalls I encountered and to build a future that's not only profitable but deeply fulfilling for all.

If you're a contractor who's tired of feeling overwhelmed by the seemingly endless challenges, who wants to take control of your business and build something that can *actually* last, I invite you—no, I *urge* you—to sign up for his monthly newsletter. You'll be the first to know when the course launches, and you'll gain access to exclusive resources, tools, and insights that can help you transform your operations. I promise it won't be just theory. It's sure to be a practical, down-to-earth guide to turning your hard-earned lessons into actionable steps for success.

All I can really say now is that I'm thankful—not just for the success we've achieved, but for everything that brought me here. Every mistake, every problem, every painstaking hour of rebuilding has shaped me into a better leader. And—at least I'd like to think—a better person.

To every construction business owner out there struggling with the same challenges I once faced: know that you're not alone. Timothy is out there, helping those of us that need a little push in the right direction. Learn to embrace your failures as mere stepping stones, invest in your team, and never stop learning. With a clear vision, the right tools, and a dedication to an honest living, you can build a future that's not just profitable but truly rewarding.

www.ingramcontent.com/pod-product-compliance
Lightning Source LLC
LaVergne TN
LVHW010655110826
845149LV00014B/3103
* 9 7 9 8 9 9 9 7 2 3 2 1 5 *